Loot, Legitimacy and Ownership

Duckworth Debates in Archaeology

Series editor: Richard Hodges

Published

Debating the Archaeological Heritage
Robin Skeates

Towns and Trade in the Age of Charlemagne
Richard Hodges

Loot, Legitimacy and Ownership
Colin Renfrew

Forthcoming

Archaeology and Text
John Moreland

Beyond Celts, Germans and Scythians
Peter Wells

Loot, Legitimacy and Ownership

The Ethical Crisis in Archaeology

Colin Renfrew

Duckworth

This impression 2006
First published in 2000 by
Gerald Duckworth & Co. Ltd.
90-93 Cowcross Street, London EC1M 6BF
Tel: 020 7490 7300
Fax: 020 7490 0080
inquiries@duckworth-publishers.co.uk
www.ducknet.co.uk

A catalogue record for this book is available
from the British Library

ISBN 0 7156 3034 2
EAN 9780715630341

Printed and bound in Great Britain by
CPI Antony Rowe Ltd, Eastbourne

Contents

Contents

Illustrations

Text Figures

1. Central roundel of the 'Hunting Plate' from the Sevso Treasure (p. 47).
2. Chart indicating how the Salisbury Hoard was dispersed from the detectorists to their dealer and so through a network of dealers and auction houses to museums and private collectors in Britain and overseas (p. 88).

Plates (*between pages 64 and 65*)

1. Silver drinking horn, believed to have been looted from Iran. Now in the collection of the Miho Museum, Japan, and recently exhibited in the Antiquities Museum, Leiden.
2. Roman fresco of unknown provenance from the Fleischman Collection, now in the Getty Museum.
3. Silver bowl from the 'Lydian Treasure', returned by the Metropolitan Museum of Art, New York, to the Turkish Government after legal action was brought in the New York court.
4. The two parts of the 'Weary Herakles', a Roman statue found at Perge. *Upper*: Jointly owned by the Boston Museum of Fine Arts and the collectors Leon Levy and Shelby White; *Lower*: Antalya Museum, Turkey.
5. The Getty Kouros: of doubtful authenticity and unknown provenance, purchased with a bogus authentication in the name of a deceased classical scholar.
6. The Sevso Treasure, a collection of Roman silver of unknown provenance, the subject of two legal actions and an out-of-court settlement said to be in excess of £15 million.
7. Gold 'protector' of the Moche culture of Peru, looted from Sipan and recovered by the FBI in Philadelphia.
8. Statue in Angkor Wat, Cambodia, the head removed by looters.
9. Before and after: damage to a statue of the god Vishnu in Nepal.
10. Objects from the looted Salisbury Hoard, an important group of bronze objects buried in the second century BC looted by metal detectorists and dispersed via the British antiquities trade.

7

This book is dedicated to all those individuals in every part of the world who value our shared knowledge of the human past more highly than the personal ownership of antiquities.

Introduction

Crisis is not too strong a word to use when we speak of the predicament which today faces the historic heritage in nearly every country on earth. The world's archaeological resource, which through the practice of archaeology is our principal source of knowledge about the early human past, is being destroyed at a formidable and increasing rate. It is destroyed by looters in order to serve the lucrative market in illicit artefacts through which private collectors and, alas, some of the major museums of the world, fulfil their desire to accumulate antiquities. Such *unprovenanced* antiquities, ripped from their archaeological context without record (and without any hope of publication), can tell us little that is new. The opportunity is thereby lost for them to add to our understanding of the past history and prehistory of the regions from which they come, or to our perception of the early development of human society. In nearly every country (including Britain) the pace of depredation is beyond the control of the government or of local authorities. In some countries (including Britain) it is not even effectively prohibited by law. In many countries (including Britain) the import and public sale of antiquities which have been looted and then illegally exported from their country of origin is officially sanctioned. And so the art markets of the world, in Geneva and Zurich and London and New York, continue their profitable sideline of dealing in unprovenanced antiquities. This iniquitous trade today by association brings discredit upon

9

the legitimate dealing in more recent works of art and other collectibles. Many of the police forces of the world are now concerned at the extent to which the trade in illicit antiquities is increasingly linked with money laundering and the traffic in drugs.

It seems strange that the deliberate destruction of the world's archaeological record in this way should awaken so little academic or public interest and anxiety. I find it an irony that in many countries the field of rescue archaeology or salvage archaeology is a well-developed one, involving the expenditure of many millions of pounds or dollars per year towards the mitigation of destruction, and yet that this equally destructive process of looting is the focus of so little attention (but see Meyer 1973; Tubb 1995; O'Keefe 1997).

I find it strange also that the collection of unprovenanced antiquities by wealthy private individuals is still widely considered a socially acceptable undertaking, and that reputable scholars are willing to contribute to the published catalogues when such assemblages, replete with looted antiquities, are given public exhibition by public institutions, although I myself must plead guilty to having done so in the past (Renfrew 1991). These institutions should know better than to allow such dubious artefacts to darken their doors.

My motive in writing this book is to seek some greater national and international recognition of a problem which can, I believe, only be solved or at least ameliorated if the academic community defines a common viewpoint and sense of purpose, and then proceeds to persuade the great museums and academic institutions of the world of its view. All the major and ancient museums of the world have in earlier centuries obtained large parts of their collections by means that would today be considered dubious. But this book is not about repatriation undertaken in restitution of earlier wrongs, although that topic is touched on in Chapter 7. It is about stopping the looting now, and it takes the year 1970 as its somewhat arbitrary dividing line. The appropriate viewpoint today, as I shall seek to persuade you, has to be that neither institutions nor private collectors should any more purchase antiquities which are without secure and documented provenance. In pursuing such a policy it is in general prudent to follow the principle that unprovenanced antiquities are likely to be looted antiquities. In the light of the gravity of this matter we have, at the McDonald Institute in Cambridge, set up an Illicit Antiquities Research Centre to address these issues. Our periodical publication *Culture without Context* (which can be obtained from the Institute or consulted on:

http://www-mcdonald.arch.cam.ac.uk/IARC/home.htm)
is, we hope, a step in the right direction.

The time is ripe, I believe, for a review of the situation. There are indications that many international organisations (although not yet the United Kingdom Government) are taking their obligations in this field more seriously. Moreover the recent out-of-court settlement in London on the Sevso Treasure case, in which the Marquess of Northampton sued his former solicitors Peter Mimpriss and Allen & Overy for failure, among other things, to exercise due diligence on his behalf, and received a sum in settlement reputed to be in excess of £15 million (Alberge 1999), has implications for the market in illicit antiquities which are certainly worth considering. Moreover at the time of writing the United Kingdom Parliamentary Select Committee on Culture, Media and Sport is taking evidence on the issue of 'Cultural Property: Return and Illicit Trade'. Its report has been published (CMS Committee, 2000), and a government review is also now promised. But whether it will have any practical effect remains to be seen.

It is one aim of the present book to persuade collectors of antiquities that their conduct in purchasing unprovenanced material is not today the action of culturally sophisticated individuals displaying discrimination and taste in the accumulation of beautiful art works from the ancient past. On the contrary, they may be thought to evince the sensibility and integrity of the collector of birds' eggs who seeks to present himself as a bird lover. It is a further aim to invite museum curators to concede that they betray their trust as serious students of the past when they acquire unprovenanced antiquities or permit them to be displayed in their galleries. It is an additional aim to encourage legislators and governments to outlaw the illicit traffic in antiquities, not least by the imposition of import restrictions. And finally it is my intention to encourage readers to hold all three categories of person (collectors, curators and administrators) responsible for the destruction of the archaeological heritage which continues apace at the present time. In speaking of governments and administrators it is pertinent to report that in February 2000 the British Government announced its decision not to ratify the 1970 UNESCO Convention on the Illicit Import, Export and Transfer of Cultural Property, the principal international instrument to restrict the looting process (Appendix 1). At the time of writing no coherent explanation has been offered although the decision is now under review.

Acknowledgments

First I should like to thank the members of the Governing Board of the Stichting Nederlands Museum voor Anthropologie en Praehistorie, Amsterdam, and particularly the Chairperson, Prof. Dr. Willy Groenman van Waateringe, and the Secretary, Dr. Willy H. Metz, for inviting me to deliver the 21st Kroon Lecture in Amsterdam on 15 October 1999. This book takes as its starting point the original publication of that Kroon Lecture (Renfrew 1999). Dr. Groenman van Waateringe and Dr. Metz oversaw its initial publication by the Stichting and encouraged its subsequent development towards more extended publication here in book form. My colleagues in the Illicit Antiquities Research Centre at the McDonald Institute, Dr. Neil Brodie and Jenny Doole, have offered encouragement and support, especially in the matter of locating illustrations, and our colleagues at the Institute, Patricia Salazar and Anne Threlkeld, have given valued secretarial assistance. To the Managing Committee of the McDonald Institute credit is due for their foresight in establishing the Illicit Antiquities Research Centre. I am much indebted to Professor Norman Palmer of the University of London for legal advice, often very necessary in such matters as these, and for reading the text presented here. I would like also to thank Professor Barry Rider, Director of the Institute for Advanced Legal Studies, for earlier advice when I received a solicitor's letter at the instance of Mr. George Ortiz alleging libel, and to the University of Cambridge in the person of its Registrar, Dr. Timothy Mead, for supporting the work of the Institute's Illicit Antiquities Research Centre by engaging the assistance of distinguished libel lawyers, Wiggin & Co., ably represented by Michael Cash and Caroline Kean, to deal with the matter. I should like to thank Professor Richard Hodges for his invitation to publish this book in his series at Duckworth, and Professor Norman Hammond for his advice. In the matter of illustrations I am grateful to Mr. Ludovic de Walden of Lane and Partners and the Marquess of Northampton (Sevso), to the J. Paul Getty Museum, and to all those acknowledged in the captions to the illustrations.

1

The destruction of the past

Loot

The most significant cause of destruction of the archaeological heritage today is *looting*: the illicit, unrecorded and unpublished excavation of ancient sites to provide antiquities for commercial profit. This constitutes an unmitigated and continuing catastrophe for the world's archaeological heritage (Pérez de Cuéllar 1995, ch. 7). Its consequences are most acutely felt in those nations whose written history is relatively short but whose prehistory is rich and so far little known. In much of Africa, for instance (Schmidt and McIntosh 1996), the very opportunity of coming to know and understand the prehistory and history of a number of countries is being lost. The case is particularly acute in Mali (Sanogo 1999). But the same thing is true in South America (Watson 1999). Even in Greece, where a century and a half of systematic exploration have secured the basic outlines of Aegean prehistory, there are areas such as the Cycladic Islands where our understanding has been significantly and permanently impaired through clandestine excavation (Gill and Chippindale 1993). The problem today is worldwide (e.g. Messenger 1999; Brodie, Doole and Renfrew 1999).

What is to be done? I shall argue that there are two approaches to the problem. The first is to diminish or eliminate clandestine excavation in the countries of origin. Clearly that is no easy task. It is desirable that each nation should have strong laws protecting its antiquities and a sound and well-informed antiquities service, with well protected and well displayed national monuments, accompanied by a network of local museums centred upon a national museum. In this way the economic value of the heritage in terms of travel and tourism is of benefit to local communities, and there is less incentive to loot the heritage for private financial gain. It has to be said that in many countries this desirable infrastructure is lacking, and one of the goals of international aid should be to provide it.

The second approach to the problem is to tackle the distribution and consumption of illicit antiquities. The role of the academic community should be a clear one. It is to persuade the informed public that the purchase of unprovenanced antiquities has the inevitable consequence of funding the ongoing looting process. To the observation that there are antiquities on the market which were excavated long ago, the appropriate response may be to take an arbitrary year, say 1970, the year of the UNESCO Convention on the Means of Prohibiting and Preventing the Illicit Import, Export and Transfer of Ownership of Cultural Property (Appendix 1). It is now widely accepted in Britain that no public institution, such as a museum, should purchase unprovenanced antiquities unless it can be securely documented (for instance by adducing their publication prior to that date) that these have been publicly known since before 1970. Unfortunately the same view is not universally held by museums overseas, nor by many private collectors.

I shall argue that the private collectors of today who collect unprovenanced antiquities, and *a fortiori* the public museums which do so, are subscribing to the looting process by providing funds which both reward the looters and underwrite their further depredations. Let me say at once that no criticism is intended of collectors of modern art, Old Masters, furniture, objets de vertu, cigarette cards, Dinky toys etc.: the focus is

16

upon illicit antiquities. Moreover I shall criticise the concept of the 'Good Collector' of illicit antiquities (McIntosh 2000; Renfrew 2000), and the legitimisation of his or her role by the acceptance accorded by such organisations as the Metropolitan Museum of New York, the Boston Museum of Fine Arts and (until recently) the Royal Academy of Arts of London. If we cannot persuade such institutions as these to take an ethical line (see Vitelli 1996), then there is little hope for the still-surviving remains of our cultural heritage. Of course there will be those who, often from the self-interest of the dealer or of the established private collector, will make accusations of 'Political Correctness'. To them we shall reply that the serious politician cannot always escape the responsibility of trying to be correct, and respond with Richard Elia's arresting battle cry (in the context of illicit antiquities: Elia 1993): 'Collectors are the real looters'.

The role of the early collectors

There can be no doubt that, in the history of western taste, serious collecting preceded and encouraged serious scholarship, and both came well before the development of the techniques of field archaeology. During the Italian Renaissance classical statues were keenly prized by the princes of the day, and the Belvedere of the Vatican was soon followed by other collections and private museums in the cities of Italy and beyond (Haskell and Penny 1981). At about the same time Cabinets of Curiosities were formed which contained extensive ethnographic collections in addition to antiquities (Schnapp 1996). The passion for collecting motivated early excavations of a fairly organised nature, but also the activities of clandestine diggers, the *clandestini* or *tombaroli* whose activities in Etruria were lamented by George Dennis in the middle of the nineteenth century (Dennis 1848).

17

Already by the late eighteenth century the great national collections were being formed: the British Museum was founded in 1753 with the acquisition by the nation of the private collection of curiosities and of manuscripts formed by Sir Hans Sloane. Soon the great imperial powers were accumulating antiquities from the territories under their influence, so that the Parthenon Marbles of Athens are mainly to be found in the British Museum, the pediments for the Aphaia Temple on Aegina in the Munich Glyptothek, the Assyrian lions and reliefs from Khorsabad along with the Law Code of Hammurabi in the Louvre, the sculptures from the Mausoleum at Halicarnassus in Berlin and so forth. Naturally the source nations in each of these cases now talk in terms of restitution. But in each case there is no doubt that these early acquisitions were accompanied by or at least stimulated great scholarship. Indeed some of these acquisitions were associated with the birth of field archaeology – such as the finds of Layard at Nineveh (now in the British Museum), or of Schliemann at Troy (with 'Priam's Treasure' now in St. Petersburg, formerly in Berlin). The excavations were not in general clandestine and indeed often, like those at Nineveh and Troy, resulted in publications which played a crucial role in the development of the discipline. But no nation today would permit the export of its cultural treasures on such a scale.

However, since the early years of the twentieth century it has become widely accepted that each nation has the duty and right to conserve and maintain its own national heritage. Nearly every nation in the world now has its own legislation to regulate the treatment of its ancient sites and monuments, and in most cases to forbid the export, without official permit, of major antiquities originating within its borders. Since 1970 these general principles have been set in a number of international conventions, of which the UNESCO Convention of 1970 (Appendix 1) and the Unidroit Convention of 1995 (Appendix 2) are the most notable.

The nature of archaeology

Underlying these principles has been the growth of the discipline of archaeology. Since the middle of the nineteenth century it has been realised that archaeology, the study of the human past through its material remains, permits the reconstruction of the past of humankind in every region on earth. Moreover, with the aid of archaeological science, and most notably of radiocarbon dating, the systematic study of prehistory, the human past before the inception of writing and of written historical records, is making notable advances. This human history is part of the heritage of humankind, and it can be argued that the prehistory and history of every part of the world is part of our common heritage.

This perspective gives primacy of place to *information*, to the knowledge of the human past which can come about through the study of those material remains. And for a century it has been appreciated that coherent information comes about only through the systematic study of *context* – of the associations of things found within the ground where they were abandoned or deliberately buried. The purpose of archaeological fieldwork today is the recovery, generally through stratigraphic excavation, of the contexts of discovery, permitting interpretation of the economic, social and cognitive aspects of the diversity of cultures of the human past.

For that reason individual artefacts, divorced from their context, are of very much less interest and importance than they once seemed to the early collectors. Individual pieces may indeed be regarded as works of art, beautiful, interesting and evocative in their own right. But separated from their context of discovery they have very little potential to add to our knowl-

19

edge of the past. While some national governments may still take the rather chauvinist view that ownership and possession of significant artefacts (within their territorial borders) is of primary importance, most now realise that the true disaster is the illicit excavation. This results in the destruction of sites, obviously without any adequate publication, and the production of unprovenanced antiquities.

The scale of these depredations was suggested above, and it would not be difficult to document it more extensively. The essential point, however, which some private collectors still fail to grasp, is that to look after individual antiquities well, to 'give them a good home', is not enough. It is sometimes argued that when a beautiful sculpture or Greek vase (or Moche vessel, or an example of Mimbres Ware, or a Mali terracotta) appears on the market, there is some public benefit to be conferred by its purchase, so that it can be studied and put on display. But to accept that is to embark upon the slippery slope of the funding of looting and the destruction of the past. With one single exception there is no valid argument for paying money to the dealer who has funded (or rewarded) the looter or the middleman. Individual cases may be almost as painful as kidnapping: there is the temptation to 'save' the piece through purchase, just as to ransom a specific individual who has been kidnapped. But ultimately to reward the kidnapper or hostage-taker is to fund the kidnapping process. To purchase the rare bird's egg of an endangered species is, directly or indirectly, to reward the exterminator.

The single exception, and it is a difficult one, is that of the regional or national museum in the region or country of origin of the artefact (or, more accurately, of the region or country in which it was unearthed: archaeological context, and thus place of discovery, is the criterion). That is the logical repository for a looted antiquity; that is the natural 'good home'. But even there it is important not to reward the looter. In no other case does the 'good home' argument carry weight.

Of course it can be argued that if every antiquity were confined to its country of origin the wider world would never learn anything of Greek art, or Egyptian art or Maya art. It would be a pity if the culture and heritage of a country could be sampled and appreciated only by those with the means and opportunity to visit that country. This argument has weight, but it can be met by organised loans between museums, and perhaps by the authorised and legalised sale of a number of artefacts in a controlled way by the authorities in the country of origin. The old practice of *partage* on an archaeological excavation, between the overseas institutions in part funding the project on the one hand and the host country on the other, also has much to recommend it. It can certainly be argued that the decision of the Iraqi Government at the time of Sir Leonard Woolley's excavations at Ur of the Chaldees was a wise one. The most important finds were retained by the Museum in Baghdad, while rich collections went, with official approval, to the University Museum in Philadelphia and to the British Museum.

In any case there has been sufficient dissemination throughout the world of sculptures and other artefacts from many of the world's civilisations that most cultures are adequately documented today in museums well beyond those lands where their material remains are actually found.

Today the primary threat to the archaeological heritage is looting, and it is argued here that the primary need is to diminish and if possible arrest this looting process. The issue of restitution – the return to their country of origin of objects which have been in private or public collections for many years – is a different one. In most cases the matter of restitution, unless conducted within the framework of an international convention, is a political question. It is a complicated issue and will not be addressed here (see Greenfield 1995) other than in its role as a deterrent to continuing looting. Here the concern is rather with artefacts which have appeared on the market in recent years – after the year 1970, to chose the arbitrary marker noted above.

It is only through the proper study of the context of archaeological finds that it is possible to begin the task of their interpretation (Hodder 1991; Renfrew and Bahn 2000). The task can deal both with aspects of the society of the time, and with the belief systems of the day, including religious beliefs (Flannery and Marcus 1983; Renfrew 1985). Very little of this interpretation can be achieved from the study of single objects taken out of context. They do not contribute to our knowledge of the past; indeed they are parasitic upon that knowledge, for they themselves can only be dated, authenticated and given any kind of interpretation by comparison with similar artefacts that have indeed been found within a coherent context.

Context v. loot: a hypothetical example:
Philip of Macedon

Dealers, collectors and even some museum curators are often reluctant to acknowledge the crucial role of context in our evaluation and understanding of the past. A great work of art, they argue, has value in its own right, and the context is a secondary issue. This view has sometimes been expounded, for instance, by experts in the field of Greek vase painting, such as Dietrich von Bothmer. For them the ancient artwork is the primary focus and all else is secondary.

To offer an example of what I regard as the dangerous fallacy of their position I should like to consider the principal Royal Tomb at Vergina in Macedonia, discovered by Manolis Andronikos in 1977 (Andronikos 1984; Ninou 1978) and recognised by him as the burial place of Philip of Macedon, the father of

Alexander the Great. The tomb contained the entire burial assemblage of a Macedonian prince: the armour, the ivory shield (in thousands of fragments) the funeral bier with ivory decoration, the gold chests (larnakes) containing the ashes of the deceased. The whole assemblage was found *in situ* in a well constructed tomb under an earthen tumulus. The façade had two impressive pillars flanking massive doors surmounted by a mural painting of a hunting scene. Within was an outer chamber with a stone cist containing a gold larnax, and in the inner chamber a whole series of objects. The larnax in the outer chamber was surmounted by a diadem of gold leaves, and contained human bones wrapped in golden cloth and a remarkable gold openwork diadem. In the inner chamber were silver vessels, several splendid items of armour, a sword in its wooden box, and an ivory shield in a circular bronze container. A wooden bed had decayed but its ivory decorative panels were in part preserved. Within another marble cist was a larger gold larnax again surmounted by a golden diadem.

Several arguments led Andronikos to conclude that this was the tomb of Philip himself. First, the partly cremated bones within the larger larnax in the inner room gave indications of a man who had been blinded in one eye, and who was lame. Secondly, the bronze greaves among the armour indicated a man longer in one leg than the other. Both these details fitted the historically known circumstances of Philip. Thirdly, the wealth of the gravegoods indicated a noble of very high standing, very possibly of royal status. And finally, the ivory decorations of the bed or bier included what could be identified as portraits of Philip and his son Alexander, whose likenesses are well known from other representations, including those on coinage. One of the most successful aspects of the excavation was the successful restoration of the ivory shield, found in numerous small fragments and brilliantly reconstructed.

Consider however the situation which would have arisen if

this tomb at Vergina had been discovered first by *archaiokapiloi* (looters), and the objects from the clandestine excavation had been exported in some container to the north, finally reaching Switzerland. When objects are looted, all reliable context disappears, and it is likely that the objects would have been sold individually. The scraps from which the great ivory shield was reconstructed would have been overlooked. The arguments of attribution to Philip could not have been made. The assemblage as a whole and its association with Vergina would have been lost. Instead one would have been left with a number of isolated but rather special items occurring individually on the market. The splendid gold-decorated breastplate and helmet of a nobleman would be important items for sale. Above all the solid gold caskets would prove valuable items. The entry in the auction catalogue in Zurich, London, or New York might read:

A highly important *larnax* of solid gold, of Hellenistic date and of Macedonian workmanship, with applied and inlaid gold rosettes, supported by four lion's legs. Found in Macedonia, Thrace or the Euxine Coast, reportedly during the First World War. The property of a gentlemen, acquired from a distinguished Greek family in Alexandria.

The imprecision in the text as to place of origin would be deliberate, since no nation could then reliably claim ownership. The suggestion of early discovery, impossible to contradict by means of documentation, would place the find well before 1970, the year of the UNESCO Convention. Such a piece might well turn up in the hands of a well-known London antiquities dealer who would, of course, wish to be satisfied that the vendor had good title. Or perhaps in New York, in the hands of a respected dealer with experience of Aegean antiquities. No reputable dealer would admit to knowingly handling stolen goods, of course, but somewhere along the line a plausible pedigree can usually be found for unprovenanced antiquities. The Getty Kouros had a purported early authentication from a distinguished (but deceased) scholar, Ernst Langlotz, who had allegedly seen it in a private collection: the documentation turned out, subsequent to the Getty's purchase, to be fake. The Sevso Treasure came to its purchaser, the Marquess of Northampton, through Peter Wilson, President of Sotheby's, along with a Lebanese export permit. The export permit was later shown to be unauthorised and without effect: the Lebanese attribution is discredited. The Euphronios Vase was purchased by the Metropolitan Museum in New York, on the recommendation of the Curator of Classical Antiquities, Dietrich von Bothmer, on the understanding that it had been kept under the bed, in fragments, in a shoe box, by a Lebanese dealer. The then Director of the Met, Thomas Hoving, later called this attribution into question, and the vase is widely believed to have been found in Etruria and smuggled out of Italy.

In recent years the concept of 'due diligence', as we shall see below, has been re-examined, and more questions are now being asked about such unprovenanced artefacts. But in the 1980s and 1990s we can imagine some major institution following the 'round robin' procedure until recently exercised by the Getty Museum (which now, however, declines to purchase unprovenanced antiquities) in contacting the Ministry of Culture of each nation from which an important object might plausibly have come and asking them if they had documentation of it. Here of course we come to the Catch 22 pertaining to all illicit antiquities. If the excavation was clandestine, followed by illicit export, the government of the source nation has absolutely no way of knowing anything about the find. The institutional buyer in our example might well contact the governments of Greece, Bulgaria, the Ukraine, Russia and perhaps Turkey (and, in view of the alleged earlier vendor, Egypt) to ensure that no government could come up with a documented claim. But of

25

course it is difficult for a government to make a claim for a clandestine find about whose circumstances it has, by definition in the case of illicit antiquities, no knowledge. This was precisely the problem, as noted below, with the Aidonia Treasure.

The purpose of this example is to emphasise how much of value would be lost to the world if the individual objects from this find had emerged, separately, one by one, and been sold at auction to one or more public or private collections. No one would be able to assert with confidence that the armour and the silver vessels belonged with the golden larnax. The human remains would have been discarded, along with the ivory scraps. The understanding that Vergina was indeed the seat of a royal dynasty would not have been documented. Any grounds for suggesting an association with Philip of Macedon would have been lost. One of the most dramatic and remarkable finds of the century would have been reduced to an auction catalogue entry with two golden larnakes and some very exceptional Hellenistic body armour.

2

Unprovenanced antiquities: the role of the private collector and the dealer

To illustrate the present dire situation in the world of archaeology and the realm of collecting it is relevant to refer to a few recent cases. Each indicates that there is something very wrong with the way the world's archaeological heritage is being treated, and that a large part of the damage is being done by those very people who are genuinely interested in that heritage and who sometimes make rhetorical statements about its significance and importance.

We shall start with three of the major private collections (Fleischman; Ortiz; White-Levy) since this may be where the nub of the problem lies, and then move on to two of the outstandingly irresponsible museums in this field (the Boston Museum of Fine Arts and the Metropolitan Museum of Art) and one whose position still seems equivocal (Getty). Two celebrated restitution cases illustrate, if only by implication, the prevalence of looting (Aidonia, Sevso). But they also show that the growing significance accorded to 'due diligence' by the courts is making much more difficult the position of the dealer or collector who tries to buy and to sell unprovenanced antiquities with 'no questions asked'.

Loot, Legitimacy and Ownership

The Fleischman frescoes

In 1994 the J. Paul Getty Museum (in association with the Cleveland Museum of Art) exhibited the private collection of antiquities formed by Barbara Fleischman and the late Lawrence Fleischman, producing a sumptuous catalogue (True and Hamma 1994). Sadly, the majority of the pieces exhibited were 'unprovenanced antiquities' – that is to say antiquities for which no documented provenance could be given, other than (in some cases) previous private collections from which certain pieces had come. As discussed earlier and also below, the year 1970 is often taken as an arbitrary marker, and if an unprovenanced antiquity cannot be documented as in a collection or museum before that time, it is widely regarded as 'recently on the market' and hence very possibly looted. On this basis a significant proportion of the Fleischman Collection must fall under suspicion. Later in this book the equivocal role of the J. Paul Getty Museum in agreeing to exhibit a collection with such a high proportion of unprovenanced antiquities is discussed. Its still more extraordinary action in proceeding to acquire the Collection has attracted criticism (Kaufman 1996) as noted below.

By way of example here, three fresco fragments of Roman date in the Fleischman Collection are chosen for comment: Catalogue Numbers 125, 126 and 127. The first, 'Vignettes of Cityscapes' (True and Hamma 1994, 251) comprises two attractive landscape scenes from the first century BC, and measures 91 by 80 cm. The second, 'Lunette with Mask of Herakles' 'matches precisely the upper portion of a fresco in the Shelby White and Leon Levy Collection and is from the same room as is catalogue number 125' (True and Hamma 1994, 251-2). The third, 'Woman on a Balcony' (plate 2) is 'probably from the upper zone of a dining room of the Augustan Period' (True and Hamma 1994, 254). Each of the three is previou: y unpublished.

28

2. Unprovenanced antiquities

So where did these three fresco fragments come from, and when, and in what circumstances? If they left Italy in the present century (and one could hardly doubt an Italian origin, perhaps from the region of Mount Vesuvius) – in the absence of other documentation – could they be other than the product of clandestine excavation and illegal export? I put the matter as a question, but it is one where the onus surely lies upon the collectors themselves and those publishing these pieces to answer (and the catalogue notes indicate that the author of these specific entries is Maxwell L. Anderson). Yet it surely is clear that these are likely to be recent discoveries, otherwise would they not be known in the literature? That careful scholar Dietrich von Bothmer can offer no further enlightenment in relation to the related piece cited from the White/Levy collection (von Bothmer 1991, 201 no. 142), although closer examination indicates that the catalogue entry here was also written by Maxwell L. Anderson.

I have chosen these pieces from the catalogue, and one could have chosen many others where the provenance is equally obscure, because at some time they have been ripped from their archaeological context, damaging the room in which they were found (and M.L. Anderson mentions similar paintings at Portici in Naples and Boscoreale, likewise in the Naples area). Is there an unreported site there which has been looted to produce what later became the Fleischman frescoes? Where did the Fleischmans acquire them and when? Were they legally imported into the United States? Can they have been other than illegally exported from Italy? If the Getty Museum now owns them, or rather has possession of them, are they considering restitution to Italy on the presumption that these are antiquities looted after 1970? These are questions that have to be asked. I may of course be wrong – it may be that the Fleischmans had some secret concordat with the Italian Government allowing them to export these items in the aftermath of an official excavation which has not yet been reported or published, and in that case I shall apologise for my alternative surmise that the ` Fleischmans purchased looted antiquities without a thorough and exacting exercise of 'due diligence'. For how could anyone buy Roman mural paintings clearly originating in Italy without in the process wondering whether these antiquities could have left Italy without breaking Italian law?

Yet the Fleischmans are introduced in the Getty *A Passion for Antiquities* Catalogue as 'Barbara and Lawrence Fleischman: Guardians of the Past' (True and Hamma 1-8). If I may add a personal note here, I regret any implied personal criticism of the Fleischmans, just as I do that of Shelby White and Leon Levy in the discussion below. I have been introduced to the latter and found them delightful to meet, and with a real enthusiasm for the pieces in their collection. I have also had the pleasure of meeting Barbara Fleischman. But I seriously doubt whether they or the Fleischmans fully understood the consequences of their actions in purchasing unprovenanced antiquities, or the condoning of looting which such purchase must in some senses entail. It is their advisors whom I would single out for criticism. First of course the professional dealers. But even more so the scholars who have encouraged them in their collecting activities and those who have accorded them facilities to put their collections on public display. That is a theme to which I shall return.

The Ortiz handle

The extensive collection of George Ortiz, which was exhibited at the Royal Academy of Arts in London in 1994, contains many very beautiful objects. Almost every piece is without a full provenance, in the sense of coming from an identified and published excavation, although a good number come from early collections and these have indeed been in the public domain since before 1970. In many cases, however, the converse is true and the catalogue citation reads either as 'unpublished' or makes reference to recent first publication, sometimes in conjunction with exhibition in a Swiss or German museum, such as the Historisches Museum in Bern. This practice of exhibiting unprovenanced objects in what are generally regarded as respectable museums, and thereby conferring at any rate an element of respectability on what would otherwise be a 'hot' antiquity (i.e. unprovenanced and of recent appearance on the market, in circumstances giving rise to suspicion of looting) does begin to seem a predictable pattern of conduct in the contemporary market for antiquities. It may be described as 'antiquity laundering'. Let me at this point make clear that I am not suggesting that Mr. Ortiz or the other collectors discussed in these pages would condone or connive at looting by funding it directly or commissioning the pillage of specific objects: what I am suggesting is that by purchasing objects that may be the result of looting they are indirectly contributing to the cycle of destruction.

My example is No. 105 from the catalogue (Ortiz 1994), the bronze spout and handle of a Greek jug or 'beaked oinochoe' of the sixth century BC which is listed as coming from Vitsa in Epirus. Good! – one at first reacts – for once an antiquity with a provenance! But further examination of the catalogue entry does not clearly indicate how this piece came to be in the Ortiz Collection or how it was acquired. And the reason that I have chosen this item for further comment, out of many splendid unprovenanced antiquities in the Ortiz Collection, is footnote 3 of the catalogue entry, which reads: 'J. Vokotopoulou has identified the body of an oinochoe, Joannina Museum 2254, as belonging to our handle.'

To quote a well-known rhyme:

31

But dat's absoid:
Da bird ain't on da wing,
Da wing is on da boid.

For if from the standpoint of Mr. Ortiz the body belonging to 'our
handle' is in the Joannina Museum, from the standpoint of the
Greek Government, surely the handle belonging to 'our oinochoe' is in the collection of Mr. Ortiz. If 'our oinochoe' came from
an excavation on Greek soil, in what circumstances did the
Ortiz handle leave Greece? Was it stolen from the excavation or
how else did it leave the site? Was there an export permit for its
departure form Greece? It may be, since this piece was first
published in 1975, as the Ortiz catalogue indicates, that it left
Greece prior to our arbitrary dividing year of 1970. But did it
leave Greece legally (since antiquities in Greece have been
protected by law since 1833)? That is a matter on which the
Catalogue is silent.

The White/Levy Herakles ('Weary Herakles')

The issue of *Archaeology* for March/April 1995 contains an arresting image (Rose and Acar 1995, 49): two parts of a statue (plate 4),
the lower part in the Antalya Museum, 'the upper half of this
statue of Herakles, now jointly held by New York collectors Leon
Levy and Shelby White and the Museum of Fine Arts in Boston'.

As the authors relate, the director of excavations at the
ancient city of Perge near Antalya in Turkey heard in 1980 of
rumours that something important had been stolen from the
site. Later that year, while excavating a Roman villa, he discovered the bottom half of the Herakles statue, as well as several
other sculptures which were complete. By 1981 the top half of
the Herakles had been acquired by Levy, who gave a half
interest in the sculpture to the Boston Museum of Fine Arts.

This same piece (i.e. the upper half) was exhibited in the

2. Unprovenanced antiquities

Glories of the Past exhibition at the Metropolitan Museum (von Bothmer 1990, 237 no. 172), 'Statue of Herakles resting, perhaps contemplating Telephos'. The catalogue entry, by Cornelius C. Vermeule III, gives the provenance as 'from the Aegean Islands or western Asia Minor'. In 1992 plaster casts of the two elements were used to demonstrate that they do belong together, and one might have expected Levy and the Boston Museum, in view of the circumstantial evidence, to restore the piece to Turkey. The Boston Museum of Fine Arts has nonetheless kept the upper half, despite the strong *prima facie* case that this was looted from Turkey in about 1980. Rose and Acar quote Robert P. Mitchell, the director of public relations of the Boston Museum as follows:

> The Museum does not acknowledge Turkey's claim to ownership. There has never been any evidence that the statue was stolen, and allegations to that effect were entirely unsupported ... Indeed the break between the top and bottom halves of the statue appears to be an ancient one, such that the top half could have been removed long ago from the territory that is now known as Turkey. In the unfortunate event that the current settlement discussions are not successful, a lawsuit would be necessary. Such a case would raise significant questions.

It may be that Mr Mitchell's analysis of the legal position is correct: the onus may be upon the Turkish Government to prove that the upper half was still in its territory after its patrimony laws were enacted earlier this century (Özsunay 1997). But given the eternal Catch 22 that it is by definition impossible to document the circumstances of a clandestine excavation or an illicit export, should not the onus be on the collector? From whom did Mr. Levy purchase this upper part of a sculpture in 1981? And where did that vendor obtain it? Should there not,

33

within the procedure of 'due diligence' be some duty of disclosure? Why is it assumed that transactions in antiquities should be clouded under some veil of secrecy or confidentiality? In my own opinion, if Leon Levy and the Boston Museum of Fine Arts are not able to document categorically that the upper part of the Herakles statue has been in private hands since before 1970, there is an inescapable onus upon them to return it.

There are, however, limited grounds for optimism in that respect. The Boston Museum of Fine Arts is well known, like the Metropolitan Museum, for its 'no questions asked' acquisitions policy (Yemma and Robinson 1997; Robinson 1998a and 1998b). And of course the Shelby White and Leon Levy Collection is rich in unprovenanced antiquities, some of them unknown to scholarship prior to their purchase for the Collection in recent decades. Two of the most conspicuous (von Bothmer 1990, nos. 173 and 174) are bronze, life-size statues of the first century BC, first exhibited respectively in 1982 at the Historisches Museum in Bern and 1982 at the Indianapolis Museum of Art, in what might appear good examples of the 'antiquity laundering' process whereby unprovenanced antiquities are given a degree of respectability by exhibition in major institutions. This second piece is stated to have formerly been in the collection of Mr. and Mrs. Charles Lipson. The *Glories of the Past* catalogue entry (by M.L. Anderson) indicates: 'It has been proposed that a series of statues stood in a *sebasteion*, or hall of the emperors, at Bubon, a site in Turkey.' It is not revealed how this piece left Turkey, nor how Anderson infers the site from which the piece allegedly came. Again the implication is clear, in the absence of documentation of its earlier existence, that it may have been looted and illegally exported, although (as in the case of the Weary Herakles) in the absence of a convention of disclosure one cannot altogether exclude that it may have reached Mr. and Mrs. Lipson from an older private collection.

A common procedure for some of the more recent collectors is the production of an impressive, lavishly illustrated catalogue of an exhibition of the collection held at some complaisant institution, such as the Metropolitan Museum of Art. It is widely recognised in the antiquities trade that such an exhibition adds greatly to the commercial resale value of a privately-owned collection. And many of the major private collectors see the ideal ultimate destination of the collection as a major and well-known museum. Their benefaction may well be richly rewarded with tax deductions carefully arranged (sometimes in the past with inflated valuations) with the help of the institution in question, whose resident specialist often in fact writes the catalogue. Some museums, including the Getty, have regarded the publication of the collection in such a volume as a mark of legitimation. Indeed the full scholarly treatment sometimes amounts to academic laundering, making the acquisition of unprovenanced and possibly looted antiquities somehow less offensive: 'Provenance through publication' as one critic has commented. The titles of these lavish and often highly subsidised volumes often give off an aura of discernment, discrimination and good taste: e.g. *The Art of the Absolute* (the Ortiz Collection), *A Collecting Odyssey* (the Alsdorf Collection); *Glories of the Past* (the Shelby White and Leon Levy Collection); *A Passion for Antiquities* (the Fleischman Collection, now owned by the Getty Museum).

Wealth, status and good taste often go hand-in-hand among the cocktail parties and gallery private views of Manhattan and Malibu.

The commercialisation of the past: dealers and auction houses

Dealers are middlemen. They would not exist if there were not both a demand (the museums and private collectors) and a supply (the flow of unprovenanced antiquities from looted archaeological sites). In general both dealers and auction houses seek to clothe themselves in a mantle of respectability, and in some fields, such as the sale of Old Masters or of antique furniture, such respectability is perhaps warranted. It is only a few years ago, for instance, that the two leading London auction houses, Christie's and Sotheby's, had as their chairmen the Lords Carrington and Gowrie respectively, both former Conservative cabinet ministers.

The underlying problem so far as antiquities are concerned is that the supply of legitimate antiquities is minimal. Very few countries currently have a system whereby antiquities of limited importance, once legitimately excavated and published, may be legally sold, although this has been advocated by some serious commentators (O'Keefe 1997). And while there are a few important early collections in private hands, their dispersal by sale are rare events. One such a few years ago was the Castle Ashby sale of a collection of Greek vases formed a couple of centuries ago by an ancestor of the present Earl of Northampton (of Sevso fame), and sold by the latter to pay the bills for the upkeep of his stately home.

As a result the bulk of the antiquities offered for sale by dealers are unprovenanced. And although the apologists argue that some of these pieces come from modest private collections formed years ago (the 'grandmother's attic' syndrome), it is clear that the greater part of them come from the recent looting of excavations. Nothing could be more telling, for instance, than the extraordinary flow of Chinese antiquities in recent years, most of them passing through Hong Kong. Few British or American grandmothers had access to Chinese antiquities prior to 1970. And those that did were more likely to be collecting porcelain – Ming vases and the like – than figures and ceramics of the Han and Tang dynasties. These could only have been preserved complete if buried in tombs, from which they have subsequently been removed.

2. Unprovenanced antiquities

If the façade of respectability is to be preserved it is consequently necessary that the provenance of pieces offered for sale should not be seriously questioned. Dealers therefore generally decline to indicate from whom they have acquired a piece offered for sale on the grounds of 'client confidentiality'. In reality it is not clear why a vendor should seek to conceal his or her identity unless the object in question has been illicitly obtained or unless there is a motive of tax evasion. Of course the antiquities dealers and auction houses have a number of 'Codes of Practice' in which the utmost probity is claimed. Indeed I do not doubt that nearly all dealers genuinely try to avoid selling objects that have been *stolen* – that is to say removed from the collection of an individual owner or a museum. The case of looted objects is very different, however: these have been clandestinely removed from the ground and have never had an effective owner, even if the landowner at the time of the removal is in a legal sense the owner of such goods. In many countries the law determines that it is the state itself which is the owner of buried antiquities, but the state as rightful owner is the last to hear of it when they are illicitly exported.

Thus although the dealers will pledge that they never knowingly sell looted antiquities, they are able to use the obvious Catch 22 in this field that looted antiquities rarely come with an indelible label attached declaring them to be such. But most dealers will quite happily sell unprovenanced antiquities without enquiring too closely as to their ultimate origin, and many will resist any attempt to make public and transparent their sources of the material.

A good example was offered a few years ago by the London auction house Sotheby's. They offered for sale a series of fragmentary Early Cycladic marble figurines, dating from around 2500 BC, which they plausibly identified as coming from the 'Keros Hoard'. Keros is a small islet in the Cycladic islands which was extensively looted in the 1950s and 1960s, and it is extremely unlikely that much material left it prior to the discovery by *archaiokapiloi* (looters) of the rich site at Dhaskaleio Kavos on Keros. Thus, if the catalogue entry is correct, these objects must have been exported from Greece in the past 50 years and in direct contravention of its antiquities laws. But when this was pointed out to Sotheby's by the Greek Embassy they declined to halt the sale, and the temporary injunction granted by a London judge was not upheld on the grounds that the material had been publicly exhibited some years before at the Badisches Landesmuseum in Karlsruhe, and that the Greek Government had made no protest at that time.

The dubious dealings of the Antiquities Department at Sotheby's were graphically exposed by Peter Watson in a television documentary some years later, and then in his revealing account *Inside Sotheby's* (Watson 1997). Sotheby's subsequently discontinued their antiquities sales in London, and appointed a Compliance Officer to ensure that their internal code of conduct was more strictly observed. But other auction houses in London, including Christie's, Bonham's and Phillips, continue to sell unprovenanced antiquities. Sotheby's continues to do so in New York, which suggests perhaps that their ethical principles may be subject to some degree of regional variation. The opacity and concealment associated with the transactions of many dealers have been criticised in a recent report (Brodie, Doole and Watson 2000).

3

Causes for concern: illegitimate acquisition and reluctant restitution

Unfortunately it is not only the private collector who today acquires unprovenanced antiquities without inquiring very carefully into the legitimacy of the purchase. The Getty Museum, whose acquisition policies had been subjected to much criticism, purchased its now-famous *kouros* in 1983, and in doing so paid what was probably the largest sum even expended upon what may ultimately prove to be a fake antiquity. But the Getty has since then taken significant steps to develop a coherent and ethical acquisitions policy, even if its subsequent exhibition and then acquisition of the Fleischman Collection suggests that its ethics may still be in some disarray. Two other museums mentioned in this chapter would appear either not to have such a policy, or to apply it in such a way as to render it in practice meaningless. The law courts are now showing a more acute sensitivity to some of the issues involved, however, and the issue of the 'due diligence' to be exercised by collectors and dealers in the acquisition and sale of antiquities has become a hot one, as the cases discussed in this chapter illustrate. Most of them did not actually come to judgement, being settled out of court. But the courts nonetheless played a significant role: the preliminary judgement of the court in the case of the Lydian Treasure, requiring the Metropolitan Museum to comply with 'disclosure' requirements, would have obliged it to reveal just what the Museum knew at the time the Treasure was purchased. It may be surmised that such disclosure would have shown the Museum in its true colours, and settlement seemed the easier path. In the Sevso case (discussed in detail below, pp. 46-51) it would seem that the highly respected firm of London solicitors Allen & Overy was prepared to settle out of court, paying a sum believed to be in excess of £15 million to the Marquess of Northampton. The terms of the settlement have been kept confidential at the wishes of the defendants. One may surmise that there were aspects of their conduct in this case which they were very anxious should not be made public.

In most of these cases it is the antiquities dealers and the auction houses who play a key role, although it is one which is often overlooked.

The Getty Kouros

The Getty Kouros, a life-sized statue in the Greek archaic style in the well-known 'kouros' position, and purportedly dating from the sixth century BC, was imported into the United States, to the J. Paul Getty Museum, in 1983 (plate 5), accompanied by documents that claimed it had been in the collection of Dr. Jean Lauffenburger of Geneva since the 1930s. Its authenticity was soon questioned, and continues to seem highly dubious. Indeed it has seemed much more dubious since the discovery of a second piece, undoubtedly a fake, which has a number of similarities with the Getty Kouros. The whole issue was reviewed at a symposium held in Athens in May 1992 (Kokkou 1993) when the kouros was present in person, so to speak, having been imported to Greece for the purpose, later being re-exported back to Malibu.

It is my private assessment, on the basis of the sequence of events (rather than any expertise in archaic statuary) that the

3. Causes for concern

Getty Kouros is a fake, and that the Getty were taken for a ride to the tune of several million dollars. But in the context of the present discussion it is interesting to consider the sequence of events on the premise that the kouros may be genuine. How could the Getty Museum respectably purchase so important an antiquity, which had certainly not been documented as known to scholarship through publication prior to 1970? Is it really likely that an entire kouros could have been in private hands, in a Swiss collection, since 1930, and yet be entirely unknown to the scholarly world? Was not the Getty falling into the position familiar among acquisitive museum curators of accepting any purported documentation without asking very searching questions? Such, clearly, was the position of the Metropolitan Museum when they purchased the Euphronios Vase on the basis that it had spent the Second World War in a shoe box under the bed of a Lebanese antiquities dealer.

That suspicion is in part confirmed by the circumstance that at the time of purchase the Getty had been provided with photocopies of letters to Dr. Lauffenburger indicating that the kouros had been seen by a variety of people, including the great scholar of Greek sculpture, Professor Ernst Langlotz.

> Unfortunately, when we tried to procure the originals of these letters, we were told they had disappeared. Then, when these photocopies were subjected to the scrutiny of a German expert in typewriters, postal codes and other means of verification, they proved to be cleverly manufactured composites. The Langlotz letter in partitular could be shown to be a forgery because, although the letter is dated 1952, the postal code on the letter head did not come into existence until 1972. The association with the Lauffenburger collections thus appears to have been a clever hoax, and the real modern history of the statue prior to 1983 remains a mystery (True 1993, 13).

But this bald statement opens more questions than it answers. It seems that the kouros was not purchased from the Lauffenburger Collection directly. So from whom did the Getty purchase it? Did they really believe that so important an antiquity had been in private hands since 1930 without becoming known to scholars? And if it was a recent find, was it not clearly the product of clandestine excavation, either in Greece or Southern Italy/Sicily, and of illegal export from one of these two countries? Indeed would the same not be true even if it had been in Switzerland in 1930?

Also, on the hypothesis that the kouros is genuine, I find it strange that the Greek Government should permit it to enter Greece for a Colloquium in 1992, and even more strange that it should be permitted to leave subsequently. If the kouros is genuine it has almost certainly been exported from Greek lands (although the Italian possibility is there) and since the first enactment of Greek antiquities legislation was in 1833, such export was illegal. Why did the Greek Government not impound the kouros? As we shall see below, national governments all too often acquiesce in compromises where antiquities are concerned, although the Turkish Government has recently secured some notable successes by taking a firmer line, as is well documented by the case of the Lydian Hoard.

The Lydian Hoard

The case of the Lydian Hoard is of interest for two reasons. In the first place, it represents a noted success in the battle against looting, in that a body of looted material unethically purchased by an important public institution was returned to its country of origin after successful legal moves by that country. And secondly it illustrates the acquiescence of certain museum curators in the trade in illicit antiquities, and their complacency in the face of evidence of looting. The story has been well told

3. Causes for concern

by Kaye and Main (1995) and indeed by Rose and Acar (1995). In the mid 1960s, tumuli in the Ushak region of west-central Turkey, reputed to contain treasures dating from the age of the legendary King Croesus of Lydia, were broken and looted by villagers. Between 1966 and 1970 many of these objects were acquired by the Metropolitan Museum of Art in New York (plate 3).

Yet although rumours of the acquisition circulated, the purchase was not announced by the Museum. It was not until some of the pieces were put on permanent display in 1984 as part of the so-called 'East Greek Treasure' that the Republic of Turkey was able to conclude that these pieces were indeed those looted from the Ushak tombs. It took legal action in the New York courts in 1987, which the Museum sought to have dismissed through the statute of limitations. However in the case of *The Republic of Turkey v. The Metropolitan Museum* the Court followed earlier rulings that the purported owner of a work of art must have exercised due diligence at the time of its acquisition and the motion to dismiss was denied. The pre-trial discovery process now began and proved critical to the development of the Republic's case:

> The documents produced by the Metropolitan in response to the requests by the Republic revealed what the Metropolitan officials knew at the time they purchased the Lydian Hoard antiquities. The process itself compelled the Metropolitan to confront the damning nature of its own documents (Kaye and Main 1995, 152).

The Museum quickly settled out of court and returned the objects to Turkey (Özgen and Öztürk 1996).

It now seems clear that in this case the museum authorities knew at the time of purchase that they were buying antiquities which had been looted from Turkey only a few years previously. As Kaye and Main report (1995, 151), a former director of the

43

Metropolitan, Thomas Hoving, has said that the Metropolitan's acquisition of the Lydian Hoard objects was a prime example of the 'age of piracy' in the museum community, an era which he says ended in the early 1970s. But although some museums are formulating more careful acquisitions policies (see Appendix 1 and Appendix 4) it seems clear from the case of the Boston 'Weary Herakles' reported above that this is not universally the case. Moreover the action of the Metropolitan Museum in agreeing to exhibit the Shelby White and Leon Levy Collection, like that of the Royal Academy of Arts in exhibiting that of George Ortiz and the Historisches Museum in Bern in exhibiting unprovenanced antiquities, shows that museums are still willing to legitimise the acquisitive activities of collectors without asking serious questions about provenance.

The Aidonia Treasure

There are at least some signs that government actions by the source countries are becoming increasingly effective in blocking the public sale of recently looted antiquities, and in securing their restitution. Another excellent example is that of the Aidonia Treasure, a splendid collection of Mycenaean jewellery and other materials which could only have come from a cemetery in Greece dating to the Mycenaean period (Demakopoulou 1996). They were offered for sale in 1993 in a catalogue published by the New York dealer Michael Ward. It may be said in his defence that he had tried the time-honoured Catch 22 strategy of writing to the relevant Greek Ministry and asking if they had evidence that the material was looted. Of course, by definition, they had no direct knowledge of the material, and said so. But when the catalogue was published, it was realised in Greece not only that the collection must derive from Greek lands, but that the similarities with finds made during the systematic and authorised excavations at Aidonia made it almost certain that the Ward material had come from tombs in the area which were known to have been recently looted.

The Greek Government took legal action in New York to recover the material. The case ended in an out-of-court settlement, whereby the Treasure was assigned by Ward, without payment, to a United States based charity, the Society for the Preservation of the Greek Cultural Heritage, which undertook to return them to Greece after some lapse of time and did so after two years. It is rumoured, however, that Ward was able to achieve pecuniary advantage through the gift in the form of tax relief on the grounds that this was a 'charitable donation' – no trivial matter since the original asking price for the collection was $1.5 million. Ricardo Elia (Howland 1997, 51) pertinently asks why Americans' tax dollars should be used to reward a dealer in looted antiquities, and points out that the recovery of the objects does not recover the information lost when they were looted. Indeed it is relevant to observe that some governments seem to show more concern for questions of ownership than for information. As noted earlier, the important loss when looting occurs is indeed the loss of information as to context. The final destination of the material is ultimately a secondary consideration. As Elia points out, the main value of repatriation is the role it may play in repressing the market and discouraging future looting.

This question of tax relief is a critically important one. It is simply against the public interest, at a global level, that collectors of unprovenanced antiquities should obtain tax relief in relation to their subsequent disposal.

Disquietingly, it emerges that Ward is a member of the US Government's Cultural Property Advisory Committee, established when the Convention on Cultural Property Implementation Act was signed into law in January 1983, implementing the 1970 UNESCO Convention (Rose 1993).

There are clearly ethical issues here which the United States Government has not yet tackled.

The Sevso Treasure

One of the most notable 'causes célèbres' in the field of illicit antiquities in recent years has been the Sevso Treasure, which has been at the centre of two court actions, one in the United States (New York) – an unsuccessful legal attempt at restitution – and one in England (London). The final conclusion, reportedly a massive out-of-court settlement, may discourage the sale of illicit antiquities without the exercise of due diligence, by vendor as well as buyer. The magnificence of this collection of late Roman silverware (fourteen pieces plus a bronze cauldron in which they were alleged to have been found) is evident from the splendid sale catalogue (Sotheby's 1990) in which the Marquess of Northampton was identified as the owner (plate 6).

The Treasure, dating from the late fourth or early fifth century AD and, as the catalogue states, 'said to be found somewhere in Lebanon in the 1970s', takes its name from that of the original owner decoratively inscribed on the great Hunting Plate (Fig. 1), one of three beautifully decorated plates in the find. Along with these was an amphora, five decorated ewers, two situlas, a basin and a toilet casket, some with impressive figured decoration in repoussé work. The find is rightly regarded as one of the most important from the ancient world, to be compared with the treasures of Kaiseraugst and Mildenhall, but greater in size and weight than these. It has been suggested (Eddy 1998) that the Marquess of Northampton hoped to obtain £40 million through the sale. The treasure has been fully documented in a substantial publication (Mango and Bennett 1994), although one may question the ethical position of scholars who publish scholarly evaluations of looted materials prior to their being offered for sale.

Fig. 1. The central roundel of the 'Hunting Plate' from the Sevso Treasure, bearing a dedication to the original owner: 'Let these, O Sevso, yours for ages be, small vessels fit to serve our offering worthily.' (From Mango and Bennett 1994, 83, fig. 1-38a. By kind permission of the Marquess of Northampton.)

The earlier history of the Treasure is decidedly murky. Several pieces had been acquired in the early 1980s by the late Peter Wilson, then President of Sotheby's, for his company Art Consultancy Ltd. He prepared a document which was presented in early 1982 to Lord Northampton offering as an investment opportunity eight pieces of silver. The prospectus read: 'In 1980, farm workers in the Lebanon discovered on their land an underground chamber. This contained silver objects of the highest importance ... Until now, only eight objects have come to Europe, and all these have been purchased by the author of this note and a friend of his, an expert in early works of art' (Eddy 1998). Northampton acquired these, and others subsequently, on the understanding that they had been found in the Lebanon. Accompanying them was what purported to be an export licence from the Lebanon for this material.

It soon transpired that all was not well. Lord Northampton offered the Treasure for sale to the J. Paul Getty Museum in late 1983. The Getty, having perhaps learnt something from its experience with the kouros, was diligent and caused enquiries to be made in the Lebanon, from which it became clear that the purported export licences were bogus. The Getty declined to have anything more to do with the matter. But Lord Northampton's advisors were not daunted, and for the payment of £628,000 a fresh set of Lebanese export licences was secured. It later became clear that these licences were themselves not valid, and there is no evidence whatever that these objects were found in the Lebanon or have ever been in that country.

Following the decision to sell the Treasure at auction in Zurich, it was sent on a promotional tour to drum up interest, in the first place in February 1990 to New York. This proved a mistake, since first two and then three national governments there laid claim to the treasure. First the Republic of Lebanon on 20 February 1990 commenced an action in the Supreme Court of the State of New York for an injunction to restrain the sale of the Sevso silver and for an order that it be returned to Lebanon. Then in May the Yugoslav Government (whose interest was subsequently taken over by the government of Croatia) intervened, and then in June the Republic of Hungary was granted leave to intervene. The court case lasted until November 1993. At an early stage Lebanon abandoned its claim. Both

3. Causes for concern

Croatia and Hungary argued their case that the Sevso silver was found within their territories, but their arguments were found inconclusive, and possession of the silver was in consequence assigned to Lord Northampton, although as I understand the matter the Court did not pronounce that he had good title: it simply found insufficient the Croatian and Hungarian claims.

Already by 1991 Lord Northampton had become dissatisfied with the conduct of his solicitors in this matter – the London law firm Allen & Overy and the partner of the firm Peter Mimpriss. He changed lawyers and took the first lot to court. The Writ of Summons is a public document and is illustrated here as Appendix 7: among the heads of claim are two allegations of criminal wrongdoing, namely fraud and fraudulent misrepresentation. The crux of the case outlined by Lord Northampton was that the Sevso Treasure had by now become unsaleable, and indeed that already in 1981 this was the case in the light of the bogus Lebanese export licences. For the Sevso Treasure was not only a collection of unprovenanced antiquities: it was far from clear from what country it had come. This uncertainty could indeed form the basis for a fresh claim some time in the future. At present the argument could go that since the Treasure could have come from one of any number of countries within the former Roman empire, no one country could document that it and it alone should be regarded as the source of the silver. But fresh archaeological discoveries, for instance perhaps the location of the villa of Sevso himself, could change the picture.

In 1999 the case brought by Lord Northampton against his former solicitors was settled out of court, and it is believed that Allen & Overy and Peter Mimpriss paid damages of the order of £15 million to him (Alberge 1999). From the standpoint of the archaeologist and of those caring from the archaeological heritage this is very good news indeed in the same measure that it is bad news for dealers in illicit antiquities. For the general implication of so large a settlement must be that dealers and those advising collectors about the acquisition of antiquities must exercise, and advise the collector to exercise, due diligence. It seems that Lord Northampton was advised by Peter Wilson and perhaps by other advisors at the time he acquired the Sevso Treasure that it had come from the Lebanon legally and was accompanied by documentation to that effect. But the situation changed dramatically when the Lebanese licences turned out to be bogus, and it turned out that the matter could not be rectified simply by paying more than £600,000 for new ones.

But there are questions which remained unanswered. The journalist Paul Eddy (1998) refers to the Scotland Yard investigation in 1991, and indicates that they wanted to know on precisely what basis Peter Wilson had written in his prospectus for Lord Northampton that the Treasure had been legally exported and 'can now be sold anywhere in the world'. Since Wilson was not available – he died some years earlier – they turned to his lawyer Peter Mimpriss, the partner in Allen & Overy. 'Since he refused to be interviewed and since the police believed he must have further documents, describing what happened at key meetings with Wilson, they let it be known that they intended to arrest Mimpriss and obtain a search warrant for the law firm's offices' (Eddy 1998). The predicted arrest did not take place. As Eddy reports, Scotland Yard received a call from the Foreign Office, advising the police that in the opinion of Sir Nicholas Henderson, Britain's distinguished former ambassador to Washington – and since his retirement from the diplomatic service, a director of Sotheby's – the investigation was not 'well advised' and should be closed down. Since the reputed £15 million out-of-court settlement I have been trying, through a series of questions in the House of Lords, to ascertain from the British Government whether the police and

3. Causes for concern

the Crown Prosecution Service have had access to the documents laid before the High Court in relation to the writ seen in Appendix 7. Since the matter was settled out of court, these documents are not in the public domain, but I imagine that they could be made available to the police. So far, however, I have not succeeded in framing my questions in such a way as to obtain a clear-cut answer. The matter however seems to me one of public interest. When a well-known firm of lawyers pays a former client a sum reported to be as much as £15 million in an out-of-court settlement in a case with claims such as those of Appendix 7 in a matter relating to the acquisition in doubtful circumstances of one of the most important collections of silverware to have come down to us from the Classical world, there are grounds for public disquiet.

The public are entitled to ask just what goes on in the London antiquities market, and whether it should be more effectively regulated. In a well-publicised exposé, Sotheby's were seriously caught out in 1997 (Watson 1997) in unethical conduct, and have subsequently closed down their London antiquities auctions. This is a welcome move in itself. But the problem is an international one. It is time for us to consider the international dimension.

4

A universal problem:
Africa, Asia, America

Every continent has suffered extensive depredations in recent years to its archaeological sites, and in some cases the damage has been catastrophic. As noted earlier this has been the case for centuries. George Dennis (1848) was one of the first to complain of the effects of looting, in the case of Etruria, and Karl Meyer (1973) has very effectively placed the activity in its historical context. The early growth of the taste for collecting which has underlain the looting of archaeological sites for centuries has been well explored by Alsop (1982) and by Haskell and Penny (1981). The ethics of such collecting are increasingly called into question (Messenger 1999). The lamentable effects of such depredations in classical lands have been well analysed by Gill and Chippindale (1993) and more recently by Elia (1999). In much of the literature, as in this volume, the problem has been most widely recognised for the classical lands of Greece and Italy, along with Turkey and Egypt.

The disastrous consequences of illicit excavation in Mesoamerica were however noted long ago by Coggins (1969) and by Sheets (1978), and the long endeavours by Ian Graham to record Maya stelae in advance of the looters are well recognised (Dorfman and Slayman 1997). The appearance of Mayan antiquities in the salerooms has been examined by Gilgan (1999) and the scale of the looting discussed by Richard Hansen (1997) in his article 'Plundering the Petén'.

4. A universal problem

At a recent symposium (Brodie, Doole and Renfrew 1999) it was possible to examine these processes on a worldwide basis. It was particularly shocking to see documented the scale of damage in a number of what may be described as 'Third World' countries. In addition the scale of the problem in China was well documented (He 1999). In that country, as in many others, there is a tension between the good intentions of the central government and the lack of effective control at local level, where looting and smuggling may proceed without effective centralised control. The Miho Museum in Japan and Christie's auction house in New York have both been caught out recently with looted antiquities from China (Ruiz 2000a; 2000b). The independent observer can only wonder that any institution exercising due diligence would not suspect that unprovenanced antiquities of the magnitude reported were likely to be looted.

The ubiquity and scale of the problem revealed is alarming. To give a graphic example, Politis (1994, 12) has described the looting of a major cemetery in Jordan as a communal endeavour:

> The vast cemetery at Al Náge, with its tens of thousands of graves, has taken longer to pillage. Its sheer size and wealth of valuable objects have compelled more systematic excavations, which continue to this day. The unemployed local population has, over the years, taught itself the skill of tomb-robbing to survive. They have even learned to distinguish between Bronze Age and Byzantine antiquities. The former are described as 'Jewish' and the latter as 'Christian'.

The whole vast topic can hardly be examined in detail here, but two or three specific examples may be cited It is unfortunately true that comparable cases may be found in nearly every part of the world.

Mali and Niger: the Djenné terracottas

The looting of archaeological sites in West Africa has been particularly disastrous. As Samuel Sidibe (1995, 109f.) has asserted: 'Over the past several decades, most of Mali's cultural heritage has been removed to Europe and the United States ... Today, all regions where one may find marketable objects have been subject more to pillage than to archaeological research. This fact reveals the considerable headstart looters have over the archeologists.' Comparable comments have been made for the situation in Niger (Gado 1999) and for other West African countries, including Burkina Faso.

These words do not seem an exaggeration. For whereas the continuing looting in Greece or Italy or Mexico seriously calls into question our hope of learning very much more about the early past of these nations, at least in each case a good deal is known already through decades of systematic archaeological work. In Mali the remarkable terracottas of the Djenné culture have attracted the attention of dealers and collectors, but their archaeological context is almost entirely unknown. Over the past 25 years or so a whole chapter in the prehistory and early history of West Africa has been destroyed. To quote Sidibe (1995, 112) again in relation to a number of sites:

- In 1989, a 30 metre-long, 6 metre-wide and 80 cm-deep section of the Toguéré of Kaney Boro near Djenné was removed. The total surface pillaged was of the order of 600 square metres.
- In 1990, the Toguéré Hamma Djam near Sofara was totally disfigured by several teams of looters who moved onto the site during the rainy season.
- The same year, following the discovery of a clay statuette, the Natamatao site near the village of Thial in the Tenekou circle was literally plundered by the inhabitants

of surrounding towns. Dozens of closely-spaced wells, 2, 3, or 4 metres deep transformed the site into a veritable quarry.

- For over six years the Gao Sané site has been subject to systematic pillage by looters who settle on the site. In 1990 we visited this site which looks like a giant piece of Swiss cheese. Hundreds of wells have been methodically dug – sometimes all the way to the natural floor – and galleries linking them together have been constructed. This site belonging to the former Songhai Empire has been lost forever.

There is no doubt that one of the main objectives of the looters has been to obtain examples of the remarkable terracotta figures which, since that date, have arrived in many of the museums of the west. The loss of such material has been documented by the International Council of Museums (ICOM 1997a, 109-10). They have been widely illustrated in exhibition catalogues, even in a recent Royal Academy exhibition where national museums such as the National Commission for Museums and Monuments of Nigeria and the British Museum agreed to exhibit only on condition that recently looted materials would not be included (Phillips 1996, 489 to 495, 6.4, a to k). Of the eleven offending examples there illustrated, seven are from private collections, and one each from the Minneapolis Institute of Arts, the Musée Barbier-Muller, Geneva, the Detroit Institute of Arts, and the New Orleans Museum of Art. I presume that each of these institutions is affiliated to the International Council of Museums and is therefore in principle obliged to follow its Code of Ethics (Appendix 4). It would be interesting to learn how they can reconcile such acquisitions with their subscription to that Code of Ethics.

Nothing could more clearly illustrate the failure of ethical principles in such matters. However Mali and the United States have recently concluded a bilateral treaty (under the framework of the United States enactment of the 1970 UNESCO Convention). This treaty expressly forbids the import to the United States of such material from Mali. It is reported that the market in Mali antiquities has markedly declined in the United States since that action. But even the restitution of these antiquities to Mali could not significantly alleviate the damage which has been done. Little is known of the culture which produced them, and their contexts are for ever destroyed. A whole chapter in the world history of art has been lost to posterity.

The same observations may be made for the antiquities of Nigeria. The Louvre in Paris has recently come in for justified criticism for acquiring 1500-year-old terracotta heads from the Nok culture. Manus Brinkman, Secretary General of the International Council of Museums has commented:

> Works of this type have been banned from sale or export from Nigeria since 1943. It is a dreadful situation: the sites have been plundered to such an extent that Nigerian museums have only a very few pieces and no single complete sculpture. That means the Louvre works are by definition smuggled, and should be considered untouchable by any museum. Smuggling is now so large-scale that Africa is in danger of losing its cultural heritage altogether (Henley 2000).

Iraq: the Throne Room of King Sennacherib

One of the most flagrant and well-documented cases of looting, or perhaps more accurately of the theft, of antiquities comes from the Throne Room of the Assyrian King Sennacherib at Nineveh in Iraq. The Throne Room was first excavated by A.H. Layard and published by him in 1849. Although many of the reliefs from Nineveh were removed by him at that time to the British Museum, those of the Throne Room remained *in situ*, where they were studied and documented by the American archaeologist John Malcolm Russell in 1989 and 1990 (Russell 1998). At this point the Gulf War intervened and he has not been able to pursue his work at Nineveh.

His documentation has, however, been such as to allow him to identify without doubt a number of fragmentary reliefs from the Throne Room which have appeared on the market in Europe and the United States in very recent years. There can be no doubt that they have been stolen from the Throne Room and exported illegally from Iraq. As he writes (Russell 1997): 'Today the Sennacherib Palace site museum at Nineveh represents a world heritage disaster of the first magnitude ... This heritage disaster also highlights the role of the West as a myopic consumer of heritage, rather than cherishing it as a vanishing irreplaceable shared resource.'

It is indeed difficult to see how any dealer could buy fragments of Assyrian palace reliefs without realising that they must, almost by definition, be the result of looting. For how could they come onto the market without leaving Iraq? Of course the reliefs in question were not well published until the appearance of Russell's 1998 book, but it scarcely required such documentation to allow the secure inference that they must have originated in Iraq. Interestingly Russell himself documented one such palace relief which had a slightly more respectable provenance. It had left Nineveh in the last century and been given by Layard to a cousin in England who resided at what later became Canford School. There it had been lost to view, and then rediscovered (in the school tuck shop) by Russell. This piece was subsequently sold by the school at auction in 1994 for £7.7 million. Such a price once again underlines the motivations which drive the processes of theft (as in the Nineveh case, where the *in situ* reliefs were well documented by

Russell and clearly the property of the Iraqi state) and of looting.

The distinction drawn here between theft and looting is an important one. Ultimately to the archaeologist the theft of the Nineveh palace reliefs from the Throne Room of Sennacherib was in a certain sense less serious than would have been the looting of such materials from a clandestine excavation. For at least from Russell's 1998 book we have a full documentation of the material, which can thus make its contribution to the world's understanding of the Assyrian civilisaton. But to say that is not to diminish the sense of outrage which one feels in the face of mutilated fragments, cut down to a smaller format for convenient transportation and sale, which less than a decade earlier were integral parts of entire sculptured panels in the Throne Room. Nothing could indicate more clearly the unscrupulous nature of the antiquities trade. No doubt there may be aggrieved dealers who will read these lines and protest that they would never knowingly handle stolen objects in such a way. But in the archaeologist's book 'looted' is worse than 'stolen' precisely because it means that the excavation has been clandestine and unrecorded. These pieces were 'stolen' and the loss would have been even greater if they had not been recorded in place by Russell.

Cambodia, Thailand and Nepal

Vandalism such as that just described in Iraq is widespread in the service of the antiquities trade. Every Khmer head in the saleroom or private collection implies a headless stone statue somewhere in Cambodia or beyond (plate 8). Peter Watson has clearly documented cases in India when the looted pieces ended up in Sotheby's London salerooms (before they terminated their London sales). The flow of antiquities from Cambodia and Thailand is not dissimilar. It should be noted however that many dealers and auction houses make the distinction between 'Antiquities' and 'Oriental Art', so that antiquities from the Far East are frequently sold under the latter designation.

It is common today to see Cambodian male statues and heads in the Khmer style, often representing the Buddha and characteristically dating from the ninth to the thirteenth centuries, on sale or in auction. They correspond in general with those known to have been looted recently from Cambodia where, for instance, a number have been pillaged from the site store at Angkor (ICOM 1997b). A recent television film showed the understaffed official guardians at Angkor actually decapitating some the remaining undamaged statues which remain in position so that the heads could be removed to the comparative safety of the Dépôt de la Conservation at the site! The formidable scale of the looting process in Cambodia and in Thailand has been documented by Rachanie Thosarat. She has discussed the looting of the important prehistoric site of Ban Chiang in Thailand, and graphically described the traffic in Cambodian sculptures (Thosarat 1999, 104):

> Banteay Chmar, Cambodia is one of the largest and most important Khmer temples built by King Jayavarman VII, probably as a mausoleum for his crown prince. It is located in a remote region of Northwest Cambodia, and it is renowned for its superb bas-reliefs depicting naval battles between the Khmer and the Chams, scenes from Hindu legends and a corpus of vital inscriptions. In late 1998, units of the Cambodian army put on manoeuvres in the area to frighten off the villagers, and then moved in with heavy equipment and gutted the site of all its remaining cultural treasures for sale through neighbouring Thailand.
>
> In early January 1999, the 4th Regional Office of Archaeology and National Museums and police officers in

Prachin Bun Province arrested a lorry loaded with 117 pieces of sculpture from Banteay Chmar. The Cambodian Embassy in Bangkok reported that Cambodian soldiers delivered the reliefs in six black pick-up trucks on January 4th. These included unique carvings of two multi-armed Bodhisattava Avalokitesavaras, a Mahayana Buddhist deity. Later, archaeologists from the Fine Arts department, together with Khmer officers visited Banteay Chmar and found that those bas-reliefs came from the southwestern enclosing gallery of the temple. Prior to the theft they were in good condition. Now all 117 pieces are stored at the Prachin Bun National Museum. They have been valued at 100 million baht or approximately $2.6 million.

Similar destruction of standing monuments has recently been very clearly documented for Nepal (Schick 1998) in a moving book entitled *The Gods are Leaving the Country* (plate 9).

With its shocking series of 'before' and 'after' photographs of desecrated monuments, it is a disturbing documentation of the work of looters who are perfectly willing to destroy any monuments which they cannot successfully remove for sale.

It is studies like those of Thosarat and Schick which set in their broader context the handsome statues which appear in the salerooms or in the recently-acquired collections in western museums such as the Chicago Institute of Art (Pal 1997).

Peru: Sipan

Looting through clandestine excavation is even more painful to the archaeologist than the destruction of standing monuments, since, as in the case of the Djenné culture of Mali, whole slices of world prehistory can be lost. This has been conspicuously the case in South America, not least in Colombia, where pre-Colombian antiquities of gold have long been the objective of looters.

4. A universal problem

However, it is in Peru that the inroads made by looting have been particularly marked in recent years. The distinguished Peruvian archaeologist Walter Alva (1999) has written tellingly of the scale of the problem:

The archaeological site of Batan-Grande deserves special mention. Consisting of 30 pyramidal buildings made of sun-dried bricks and of extensive cemeteries over approximately 50 sq km, it must have been the political and religious centre of the Lambayeque or Sican culture. This sanctuary was pillaged by landowners between 1940 and 1968 who employed teams of workers and heavy machinery to open deep and wide ditches in the cemeteries close to the pyramids. The result of what could be considered the most extensive and intensive pillage in the New World left nearly 100,000 looters' pits. Part of the pillaged funerary accoutrements were sold to the 'Gold of Peru' private museum. Other pieces went to the Rockerfeller Collection or to European collections, and the ornaments damaged by machinery ended up in the melting pot. This seemingly fabulous pillage would reach its highest point with the tomb robbed in 1965 which produced 40 kilograms of gold. Dozens of vases, funerary masks and ceremonial knives, all in gold, verify how spectacular this pillage was. It can be estimated that the amazing finds at this site, now scattered all over the world, constitute approximately 90% of all archaeological gold collections attributable to ancient Peru.

Sadly the products of this looting process, which has of course destroyed any hope of understanding the cultural background from which these now-isolated artefacts came, are to be seen in museums all over the United States. The Rockerfeller Wing in the Metropolitan Museum of Art contains one of the most

61

extensive collections of ancient Peruvian artefacts in the world. Hardly any of them have any detailed archaeological provenance. It is scarcely necessary to ask how many of them left Peru legally. Nor is it difficult to grasp the enormity of the catastrophe to our potential knowledge of the past of Peru which they represent. I have not had the opportunity of seeing the 'Gold of Peru' Museum in Lima. No doubt visitors are invited to express contentment that the looted objects which it contains have remained within the territorial borders of Peru. But if that is the case it would simply represent the chauvinism which besets many national governments. In reality these pieces represent the destruction of any hope of recovering information about the past of Peru. They embody the impoverishment of Peruvian history and of the Peruvian heritage.

At Sipan, however, Walter Alva has had a most remarkable success in combating looting. Not only has he been able to excavate undisturbed royal tombs of the Moche culture, whereas hitherto all such tombs have been looted. He has, in addition, by constructing a site museum at Sipan been able to persuade the local population that controlled excavation and the legal display of the finds can bring more benefits locally than can ever accrue from the looting process. The publicity accorded to the exhibition of the 'Lord of Sipan' in the local museum has resulted in what is now a successful tourist industry, bringing considerable prosperity to the local town. This is working to the continuing benefit of a good number of the local population and contrasts with the limited gains, concentrated in just a few hands, which formerly came to the looters. Indeed the success has been so conspicuous that other settlements in the region have been asking how they too can have their own archaeological 'Lord', so as to have some share in the touristic benefits now brought to his locality by the 'Lord of Sipan'. The story of the discovery of Sipan is a dramatic one (Nagin 1990). The site of Huaca Rajada, an adobe pyramid, was first plun-

4. A universal problem

dered by *huaqueros* (looters) of the local Bernal family in 1987. The enormous quantities of gold recovered gave rise to rumours which attracted the attention of the local police, and a raid on the Bernal home produced astonishing quantities of finds, albeit only a fraction of those which had already been discovered. Alva then conducted professional excavations at the site and for the first time unearthed unplundered royal tombs (Alva 1995) which gave astonishing new insights into the Moche culture, which flourished between AD 250 and 750. At first Alva needed the protection of a considerable police presence, but gradually he managed to persuade the villagers, who at first regarded him as a government-supported thief himself seeking to make off with local treasures, that it was in their interest that the heritage of Sipan should be brought to light, and Moche history become known. Since 1993 his museum, the Museo Nacional Bruning, has developed a Programme of Protection of Archaeological Monuments. It has aided the creation of organisations of peasant volunteers who watch over the monuments in their districts. There are now eight groups with 350 members in the three valleys of the region.

The looted gold, much of which had been routed through London in view of the laxity of British law in relation to antiquities (Nagin 1990), was exported to California. There, on 30 March 1988, it gave rise to an armed raid by sixty US Customs agents. A separate seizure in Philadelphia led to the recovery of a royal gold ornament weighing 1.3 kilograms and valued at $1.6 million (plate 7). It had been smuggled into the United States in the diplomatic bag of the Panamanian consul. As a result of these enterprises the US Government promulgated an emergency law in 1990 to restrict the entry of Moche and Sipan artefacts, and a bilateral Memorandum of Understanding between the US and Peruvian Governments (within the framework of the US legislation enforcing the 1970 UNESCO Convention) now restricts the import of any archaeological material from Peru.

There are several moral conclusions to be derived from the Sipan case. One of the most important is that it is ultimately in the interest of the local population to conserve their historic heritage, which will bring more benefits in the long run than the one-off sale of some special artefacts. A second is that collectors – and those purchasing the Sipan loot included distinguished figures, members of museum boards and a Nobel laureate – should recognise the damage they cause when buying unprovenanced artefacts. The third and most important is that the world is a richer place, in the historical sense, for the information about the Moche culture, one of the most notable of pre-Columbian America, which Alva was able to derive from the excavation of the unplundered tombs of Sipan.

1. Drinking horn (rhyton), of the Achaemenid period (6th to 5th century BC), presumably from Iran. Ht. 25.7 cms. Provenance unknown. Currently in the possession of the Miho Museum, Japan, and exhibited in 1999-2000 in the Antiquities Museum, Leiden.

2. Roman fresco of unknown provenance from the Fleischman Collection, 'Woman on a balcony', 'Probably from the upper zone of a dining room of the Augustan Period' (True and Hamma 1994, 254). Now in the J. Paul Getty Museum, Malibu, California. Ht. 60 cms.

3. Silver bowl with gold appliqués, from the 'Lydian Treasure', formerly in the Metropolitan Museum of Art, New York, now returned to Turkey. 6th century BC (after Kaye and Main 1995, pl. 21; Özgen and Öztürk 1996, no. 33). Diam. 15.3 cms.

4. The two joining parts of the 'Weary Herakles', a Roman marble statue of the
second century AD, found at Perge. *Upper*: currently in the possession jointly of the
Boston Museum of Fine Arts and the Collection of Shelby White and Leon Levy
(Ht. 67 cms); *Lower*: in the Antalya Museum, Republic of Turkey (after Rose and
Acar 1995).

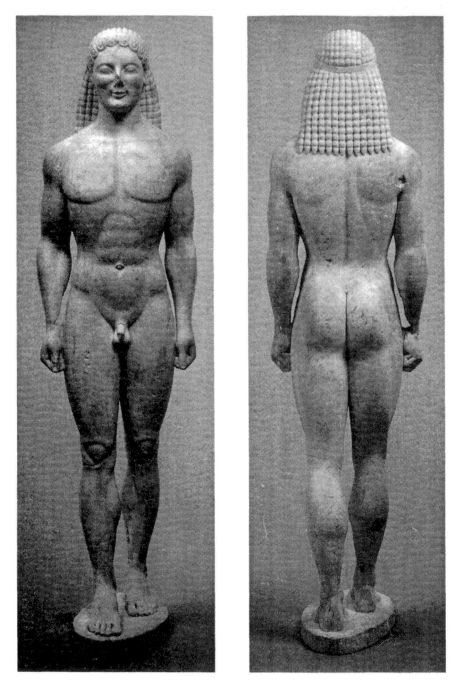

5. The Getty Kouros: life-sized marble statue of unknown provenance, allegedly of
the sixth century BC, acquired with bogus documentation by the Getty Museum in
1983, and of doubtful authenticity. Ht. 200 cms. J. Paul Getty Museum, Malibu,
California.

6. The Sevso Treasure, a collection of late Roman silver of uncertain provenance, purchased with fake Lebanese export licences by the Marquess of Northampton, as later advertised for sale in Zurich in the 1990 Sotheby's auction catalogue.

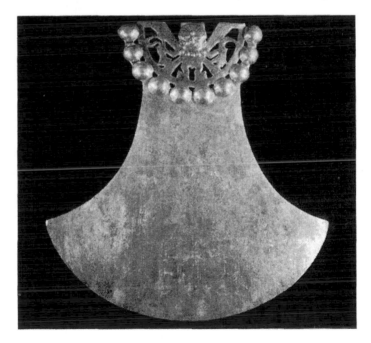

7. Massive gold 'protector', looted from Sipan, Peru and recovered in Philadelphia in the course of a raid by the Federal Bureau of Investigation (from Alva 1995, 209).

8. Statue *in situ* at Angkor Wat, Cambodia, from which the head has been pillaged by looters. 12th century AD (from ICOM 1997b, 15).

9. Before and after. Statue of the god Vishnu in the courtyard of the Bhubaneshvar Temple in Deopatan, Nepal. Ht. 45 cms. The statue was stolen in February 1986 (from Schick 1998, 78).

10. (a) Decorated bronze miniature shield from the Salisbury Hoard, sold to the British Museum by Lord McAlpine and afterwards returned by the British Museum to the rightful owner. 2nd century BC. Ht. 7.7 cms (from Stead 1998, pl. 1). Now again in the British Museum.

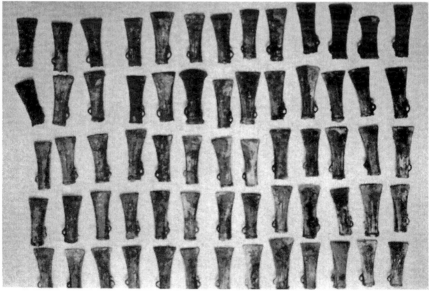

10. (b) Socketed axes of bronze age date from the Salisbury Hoard, as photographed by Brian Cavill soon after the discovery. Just one component of this extensive votive deposit which numbered nearly 600 pieces (from Stead 1998, pl. 2). Some of these are now in the British Museum, others have not been recovered following their dispersal via the British antiquities trade.

5

Ineffective safeguards
and evolving moralities

The International conventions

It is unfortunately the case that national and international legislation bearing upon the sale of illicit antiquities is weak. While most countries have legislation protecting their own heritage (and surprisingly the United States is one of the few nations in the world where it is not illegal to undertake unsupervised and unpublished excavations to recover ancient artefacts for sale, so long as the excavations take place on private land), there are in general few laws restricting the public sale of antiquities looted overseas (see Palmer 1998).

But at least there are several international conventions which express a clear view, and which can, in certain circumstances, be effective. The first of these is the 1970 UNESCO Convention on the Means of Prohibiting and Preventing the Illicit Import, Export and Transfer of Ownership of Cultural Property (Appendix 1: see Askerud and Clément 1997). It sets a framework, but is, like all such conventions, dependent upon its ratification by the relevant nations. It has not yet been ratified by the United Kingdom. But it does offer a framework for bilateral agreement between nations. It is under the aegis of such agreements between the United States (Kouroupas 1995) on the one hand and Mali and Peru (Azoy 1981) on the other, that restitution of antiquities has taken place. It is, up to

65

the present time, the principal legal instrument offering a framework by which the illicit traffic in antiquities may be restricted.

The 1995 Unidroit Convention on Stolen or Illegally Exported Cultural Objects (Appendix 2) works from a comparable perspective (Prott 1997), and in effect supplements the 1970 UNESCO Convention. It includes in Article 3.2 the following important statement:

> For the purposes of this Convention, a cultural object which has been unlawfully excavated or lawfully excavated but unlawfully retained, shall be considered stolen, when consistent with the law of the State where the excavation took place.

It is of course the case that neither of these Conventions is retroactive: they do not bear upon any actions taking place before the ratification by the countries concerned. So that collectors or museums need not fear that their existing collections might be in jeopardy if they come into effect. But this definition is nonetheless a highly important one, since it clearly indicates that good title will be difficult to achieve for an unprovenanced antiquity in such circumstances. And it underlines the need for 'due diligence' by dealers and collectors when artefacts change hands.

The position in Britain is particularly unsatisfactory. In February 1997 I asked a question in the House of Lords on this matter, to which the relevant minister (Inglewood 1997) replied:

> It is not an offence to import into this country antiquities which have been illegally excavated in and exported from their countries of origin.

5. Ineffective safeguards

In late 1997, in response to another parliamentary question, the newly elected Labour Government (one of whose first actions had been to rejoin the UNESCO organisation) announced that it was giving consideration to ratifying the 1970 UNESCO Convention, and subscribing to the 1995 Unidroit Convention. After several promptings and reminders it announced in February 2000, and without giving any specific reasons, that it would do neither. This remarkable decision leaves Britain without any public policy regulating or restricting the traffic in London of objects looted overseas. It also leaves unprotected and without any international means of redress the rightful owners of any British antiquities which are looted in this country and illegally exported, such as the Icklingham bronzes, now in a private collection in New York.

Recently a Parliamentary Select Committee, the Culture, Media and Sport Committee, under the Chairmanship of Mr Gerald Kaufman MP, held an inquiry into 'Cultural Property: Return and Illicit Trade', and its Report (CMS 2000) was highly critical of the current situation, recommending adoption by the United Nations of the Unidroit Convention. But a Select Committee has few actual powers: it simply publishes a report. On 12 April 2000, during a 'Newsnight' television interview with the author, the Minister for the Arts, Mr Alan Howarth MP announced the formation of a governmental committee to investigate and formulate recommendations on this theme. But the United Kingdom Government had just given two-and-a-half years' consideration to this matter, reaching no conclusions other than the entirely negative and unexplained decision in relation to the two principal international conventions. Perhaps something more positive will result from the new committee's work.

Meanwhile the position remains as it has been for many years: London continues to be a clearing house and staging post for illicit antiquities. To quote a recent article by K.D. Politis,

67

Loot, Legitimacy and Ownership

referring to the illicit traffic in antiquities from Jordan (Politis 1994, 15):

In July a large shipment of antiquities bound for New York was intercepted by British customs. Experts from the British Museum called in to identify the objects confirmed that they included some characteristic pottery from the Safi cemetery in Jordan. The London-based dealers who were handling the shipment claimed to have obtained a valid Jordanian export licence. Considering that only very specific archaeological institutions are ever allowed to export a very limited quantity of antiquities for study purposes, it is certain that this permit was issued illegally. But since Britain is not a signatory to the international convention prohibiting the transportation of unregistered antiquities, the shipment was allowed to leave for the US. The only thing that could be done was to alert American customs authorities. The USA has signed the convention and could stop such illegal trade.

The role of the museum

For some time now the museums of the world have given consideration to their ethical positions. One of the first to make a clear statement against looting and the collection of unprovenanced antiquities was the University of Pennsylvania Museum in Philadelphia, which reached its view already in 1970, the year of the UNESCO Convention (Appendix 3). This may be regarded as a strong statement, since it makes clear that the Museum will no longer collect unprovenanced antiquities, and that a pedigree is needed for any acquisition.

At first sight the Code of Professional Ethics of ICOM (the International Council of Museums), first adopted in 1989 and revised in 1995 (Appendix 4) is comparably stringent. The relevant paragraph (3.2) reads:

A museum should not acquire, whether by purchase, gift, bequest or exchange, any object unless the governing body ... are satisfied that the museum can acquire a valid title to the specimen or object in question and in particular it has not been acquired in, or exported from, its country of origin ... in violation of that country's laws.

Unfortunately, however, no enforcement procedures are suggested, and many museums take the weakest possible interpretation, avoiding only acquisitions which can positively be shown to be looted. Such cases are of course rare, that is why the former Getty 'round robin' procedure, mentioned above, of writing to governments in relation to a potential acquisition and asking whether they have evidence that a specific object was illegally exported from their territory, is meaningless. It sounds as if it conforms with the ICOM Code of Professional Ethics, indeed perhaps it does, but it falls far short of the Philadelphia decision.

In 1995 the J. Paul Getty Museum announced a new policy, indicating that it would acquire pieces only if these had a well-documented provenance (Cocks 1995), and putting in an additional level of requirement (in addition to that of the 'round robin' procedure):

that the piece had to have been previously documented as being in an established collection or coming from a known place that was completely legal.

Unfortunately, however, its own interpretation of this requirement is distinctly less than stringent. Little more than half a year following that announcement it illustrated the latitude of its policy by acquiring the Lawrence and Barbara Fleischman Collection, which as noted above is composed mainly of objects without provenance, many of them acquired by the Fleischmans since 1970. In very few cases has it been demonstrated that they are other than the product of looting. As one commentator puts it (Kaufman 1996):

> It is the very collection that, when exhibited at the museum, was censured by members of the archaeological community who branded it a glaring example of how the flow of illegal antiquities is tacitly condoned – indeed abetted – by members of the trade, collectors and museums. 'This acquisition is in line with exactly what we said we would do', declares Ms True, adding 'We went out of our way to be clear that we were not saying we would not buy any more unprovenanced material.'

The Getty's new position as announced in 1995 is thus not quite the radical change of policy which it seemed at first to many observers.

The British Museum has, however, for many years followed a more stringent policy, which is to avoid acquisition (whether by purchase or bequest) of unprovenanced antiquities, defined as those appearing on the market after 1970 (Appendix 5). Exception is made for minor antiquities and, in certain circumstances, for those originating from within the British Isles, for which the British Museum is the repository of last resort. But it is clear that the British Museum could not today, in terms of its policy, acquire any of the unprovenanced material from the Fleischman Collection which the Getty as recently as 1996 secured in its entirety.

Of course the Getty has a much more carefully defined position than the Metropolitan Museum of Art or the Boston Museum of Fine Arts. These are among the most flagrant public

70

5. Ineffective safeguards

institutions in the world when it comes to the acquisition of unprovenanced antiquities, profiting by the lax conditions in the United States concerning tax deductions, which allow benefactors and indeed dealers to profit from giving unprovenanced antiquities to museums. The *Boston Globe* has recently been investigating this situation (Robinson 1998a):

> But dealers seeking tax-deductions often donate artifacts to curators they sell objects to. The [Boston] Museum of Fine Arts' list of donor-dealers amounts to a 'who's who' of dealers, and some collectors, who have been involved in controversy over the origin of some of their acquisition. They include the London dealer Robin Symes, Demirjian, White and Levy and the late Lawrence Fleischman, a major purchaser of undocumented antiquities whose collection was acquired in 1995 by the J. Paul Getty Museum. Two major collectors who face claims by foreign governments seeking the recovery of artifacts are also among the MFA donors: Maurice Tempelsman, the New York financier and companion to the late Jacqueline Kennedy Onassis; and Jonathan H. Kagan, one of the defendants in Turkey's lawsuit demanding the return of the Athenian coins. Kagan has donated numerous undocumented antiquities to the MFA, including ceramic cups from the 7th century BC ... Also among the dealers who have sold classical artifacts to the museum is Robert E. Hecht Jr., a Paris-based antiquities specialist who was once declared persona non grata by the Italian and Turkish governments for his alleged role in selling plundered antiquities. Hecht, the *Globe* reported in April, played a central role in a $1.8 million sale to New York's Metropolitan Museum of Art of a 3rd century BC silver trove ....

In my own view there is little hope for the shared heritage of

71

humankind when public institutions which aspire at least to a semblance of respectability, maintain acquisitions policies which not only fail to deter looting, but through their purchases or their acceptance of gifts, seem actively to condone it.

It would be wrong to single out the Metropolitan Museum of Art and the Boston Museum of Fine Arts for exclusive criticism. It is clear that many other museums in the United States fall far short of the aspirations enshrined in the Philadelphia Declaration. The field of Asiatic antiquities, like that of Mesoamerican artefacts, is one in which ethical standards are often lax. The Art Institute of Chicago, for instance, has recently published a sumptuous and glossy volume, *A Collecting Odyssey* (Pal 1997), which illustrates numerous antiquities among other art works collected by Jim Alsdorf, Chairman of the Board of Trustees from 1975 to 1978, and his wife Marilynn, currently a member of the Women's Board of the Institute.

None of these art works is given any specific provenance in the publication. Several give rise to the suspicion that they may have been looted. Numbers 102, 103, and 106 to 114 (Pal 1997, plates 88 to 98) and several others are reportedly from 'Pakistan (ancient Gandhara)' and many others are from unspecified provenances in India, Cambodia and Thailand. I find it quite extraordinary that details of provenance and other circumstance of acquisition are omitted from this volume. Without writing to the Art Institute of Chicago one has no means of ascertaining how many of these pieces were acquired by the Alsdorfs after 1970, and how many of those (if any) were legally exported from their country of origin, accompanied by an export licence. It would be imprudent to state here without further investigation that many of these pieces have been looted. But, bearing in mind the well-documented evidence for the looting of Gandhara sites (Ali and Coningham 1998), it may certainly be suggested that the Art Institute of Chicago in this glossy publication, has done nothing to set the reader's mind at rest, and in

72

that respect falls far short of the standards enunciated in the Philadelphia Declaration of 1970.

Nor is the problem restricted to the museums of the United States, although these and their benefactors may be among the wealthiest collectors of unprovenanced antiquities.

Recently a selection of antiquities from the recently formed Miho Museum of Japan has been exhibited in selected western museums (Los Angeles 1996; Leiden 1999).

Few of these pieces appear to have any respectable provenance, or at any rate none is given in the published catalogues, and most of them are clearly recently acquired. There is, for instance, an important series of gold and silver objects dating to the fifth century BC (as well as some from later periods) which must evidently have come from Iran (plate 1). There has been no publication of the excavations which might have yielded such objects, and no announcement of any authorised export of these objects from Iran.

Once again I have not yet had the opportunity of asking the Miho Museum for details of the provenance of these objects. But it is fair to say that, when they are published without provenance in exhibition catalogues (e.g. Leiden 1999), the suspicion must arise in the mind of the reader that they may be the product of looting – of clandestine excavation and illegal export. Nor should criticism be restricted in such case to the Miho Museum as owners of this seemingly unprovenanced material. How can a respectable museum, as one imagines the Rijksmuseum van Oudheden in Leiden to be, exhibit hitherto unpublished antiquities in this way without enquiring whether they have a respectable provenance? If they do not check on this, such a museum must fall under the suspicion that it is condoning looting and the illicit traffic in antiquities. That this is no idle notion is confirmed by a report in *The Times* (Alberge and McGrory 2000) referring to:

... the 'Western Cave Treasure', discovered in Iran in the 1980s ... and illegally smuggled out of Iran to London and the West .... Part of the collection was sold to the Miho Museum in Japan. Exhibits from the Miho's collection are currently on loan to the Antiquities Museum in Leiden.

So much for the Code of Ethics of the International Council of Museums.

The academic world

When one asks what may be done to curb the looting and the traffic in illicit antiquities, there is no single, simple answer. As noted earlier, much more could and should be done in the source countries to encourage the provision of a good and effective antiquities service, and above all to ensure that the economic benefits (often through tourism) of a rich cultural heritage are adequately shared at local level.

But ultimately it is *we* the academic community and *we* the informed public, who must bear the main responsibility. I mean this in both a particular and a general sense.

In this particular sense, it should become widely understood and agreed among academics, which is not the case at present, that it is unethical and immoral to aid and abet the sale of illicit antiquities by offering authentication and expertise (see Vitelli 1996). Some archaeologists have argued that, in order to maintain that principle, they should never publish or give a citation in print to an unprovenanced antiquity. Although I have myself done so in the past (Renfrew 1991), I now feel that there is much to this argument. Indeed I would not today commit again what I now see as the ethical mistake of using a collection of unprovenanced antiquities to illustrate a discussion of a specific early period in the history of art (in this case Cycladic art), even though the collection was formed within the country of origin and with the formal permission of the government of that country. For governments simply should not condone the collection of unprovenanced antiquities, which must in many cases be the product of looting and thus of the destruction of archaeological information. It is a matter for surprise and concern that a former Prime Minister of Greece should actually form a collection of antiquities evidently deriving from unauthorised excavations (i.e. looting) in Crete and place it on public exhibition. It seems extraordinary that he should be able to do so with a permit from the Greek Archaeological Service and make the claim that the enterprise has been 'a true labour of love' on the grounds that he has been able to 'rescue precious antiquities from expatriation' (Mitsotakis 1992, 10).

Certainly I share the view that it is inappropriate for a scholar to authenticate or document an unprovenanced antiquity in such a way as may facilitate its subsequent sale. Such a view has been formulated and endorsed by the Council of the British Academy (Appendix 6), and it is to be hoped that other scholarly academies and learned societies will adopt the same position.

The scholars who offered expertise in some of the foregoing 'causes célèbres' for instance, have been criticised. Dr. John Betts (1993), who gave scholarly descriptions of the Aidonia items for Michael Ward's sale catalogue, has been criticised in Greece, and Dr. Marlia Mango, the eminent scholar who studied the Sevso Treasure, has likewise been the subject of criticism. The conservation work for the Sevso silver is understood to have been undertaken in a private capacity by Anna Bennett, based at the Institute of Archaeology in London. That association has caused embarrassment to the Institute, which no longer permits such work to be carried out on its premises. For similar reasons the Research Laboratory for Archaeology and the History of Art at Oxford no longer carries out thermoluminescence determinations: it had proved difficult to avoid their use in the authentication and marketing of unprovenanced antiquities.

But it is also our role to seek to persuade scholars more widely as to the logic and merit of this position. It is to be noted that when Dr. Dietrich von Bothmer of the Metropolitan Museum of Art was proposed several years ago for election to Honorary Fellowship of the Society of Antiquaries of London, considered a high honour in academic circles, there were protests from some Fellows concerned about the ethics of the acquisition policies which he had operated for the Museum. The Council of the Society reconsidered the matter and the nomination was withdrawn. It would not be correct to say that he was 'blackballed' in the election process since the matter did not come to a vote, but in the event he was denied Fellowship. Similarly questions have been asked in the *Boston Globe* and elsewhere about the role of Cornelius Vermeule III, formerly curator at the Boston Museum of Fine Arts, about purchases which the museum made during his time as curator (Kornblut 1998; Robinson 1998b).

Ultimately it is the collectors themselves whom we must seek to influence. Mr George Ortiz, in the preparation of his catalogue (Ortiz 1994), invited me to contribute expertise which I declined to do. As he remarks (Ortiz 1994, 42, note 1):

Faced with this Neolithic section, entries 42 to 46, the author, somewhat unsure of his dating, in view of the divergence of opinion in various publications, and wishing to approach the truth in the measure of the possible in order to advance knowledge, consulted Colin Renfrew, explaining what precedes. Unfortunately he declined to help on the ideological grounds of what the Americans call 'politically correct thinking'; in this he has been joined by Lauren E. Talalay whom we consulted as a last resort.

I hope that the underlying rationale is becoming more clear: it is not always wrong to be 'politically correct'!

On the wider front, however, the educated public must have a greater role. When it is generally understood that the collecting of unprovenanced antiquities funds the looting which is destroying our heritage, it is to be hoped that the public will react against the acquisition and display of such materials in museums. It really is not acceptable that some of these continue to behave as if they were still in an 'age of piracy', whatever may have been the situation earlier.

When it comes to collectors of illicit antiquities, the only good collector is an ex-collector (Renfrew 2000; McIntosh 2000). The 'only giving it a good home' argument may apply for stray dogs, but with antiquities it abets the looting process. There is an analogy here with the wearing of furs of endangered species and the collecting of birds' eggs. These things used to be done without anyone seeking to question them. But when the right questions are asked, such activities become increasingly difficult to condone.

As a first objective we should seek to question the process of legitimation of the collection of questionably-licit antiquities which is accorded by those institutions which display private collections of unprovenanced antiquities, and which do so with all the social éclat of a private view or a vernissage in an art gallery. There is nothing to celebrate when unprovenanced antiquities are placed on public view.

Evolving moralities

In surveying the recent history of looting and the collecting of unprovenanced antiquities it is important to recognise that we live in an age of evolving moralities. As noted above, the early collections of the world's greatest museums were formed in a period prior to the formulation of national antiquities laws.

77

Such collections were formed in a manner which would be entirely unacceptable today.

It may well be argued that the sculptures of the Pergamum Altar (now in Berlin), the Venus de Milo (in the Louvre) or the Parthenon Marbles (in the British Museum) should be returned to their countries of origin, and indeed claims for restitution have to be examined on their undoubted merits. To do so, however, might not in itself diminish the ongoing destruction of archaeological sites and the continuing looting of the cultural heritage which are our main concern here. For instance, the recent and wanton destruction of the Throne Room of Sennacherib at Nineveh (see Chapter 4) is a loss to the heritage which sadly has taken place in our own time, for commercial gain and accompanied by deliberate damage to the reliefs. Today we should be doing better.

Since 1970, the year of the UNESCO Convention (Appendix 1) and of the Philadelphia Declaration (Appendix 3) there has been a process of change and re-definition. As noted earlier, it is only recently that institutions such as the British Museum and the British Academy (Appendices 5 and 6) have produced explicit formulations of clear guidelines about these matters. It is easy, but perhaps pointless, to be censorious in judging earlier actions and decisions by the more evolved morality of today, and the 1970 UNESCO and 1995 Unidroit Conventions are not retroactive. But surely it is now time that they were generally and rigorously applied.

On the one hand there are a few encouraging signs. For example, following the unease widely expressed after it hosted an exhibition in 1994 of the Ortiz Collection, the Royal Academy of Arts decided to exclude unprovenanced antiquities from its subsequent Africa exhibition in 1996 (Phillips 1996) and, albeit with a few exceptions, succeeded in doing so. Again the J. Paul Getty Museum, after its unfortunate experience with the Getty Kouros, exercised much greater diligence in the case of the

5. Ineffective safeguards

Sevso Treasure and, in consequence, brought into the open the issue of the forged Lebanese export licences. In 1995 it announced what seemed a major step in eschewing future purchases of unprovenanced antiquities (Cocks 1995), although the following year it dismayed the archaeological world by acquiring the Fleischman Collection, composed principally of just such doubtful items, seemingly under the uncertain logic that 'publishing equals provenance' (Kaufman 1996). Such reforms and changes of position are not easy, however, and the good intentions of the Getty seem further underlined by its own initiative in returning to Italy a number of pieces apparently stolen at an earlier stage in their history, and in doing so without first being in receipt of a formal request by the Italian Government (Lee 1999). This is an important and welcome step, but in a way it highlights the distinction between *stolen* antiquities (i.e. documented as once in a known collection from which they were abstracted by theft) and *illicit* antiquities (i.e. clandestinely excavated and illegally exported antiquities, for which there is naturally no specific record). For the understanding of the past it is context which matters, and in that sense looting from the earth is much more serious than subsequent theft from a storeroom or gallery.

On the other hand, until that point is fully appreciated by museums and curators, the acquisition of unprovenanced antiquities by curators and collectors will continue to fuel the looting process. We have seen how some institutions – we have chosen the Metropolitan Museum of Art and the Boston Museum of Fine Arts for critical analysis, but they do not stand alone – have been slow to adapt to the new, evolving ethical standards of the day, and still appear to live in what Thomas Hoving has called 'the age of piracy'. Sadly, by their attitude they continue to encourage the purchase of unprovenanced antiquities by private collectors, and indeed the United States tax authorities continue to afford tax benefits on the basis of

79

benefactions of such antiquities, on a no-questions-asked basis, at the expense of the American taxpayer.

There are, however, encouraging signs that some of these important distinctions are now being understood. The United States courts are requiring higher standards in the exercise of due diligence. And national governments, notably Turkey in the case of the Lydian Treasure and Greece with the Aidonia Treasure, are using these opportunities to establish higher standards of international conduct. The damages paid to the Marquess of Northampton by those who were his advisors at the time he bought the Sevso silver, on the grounds of their failure to exercise due diligence on his behalf, are a reminder to middlemen and to dealers that they too have responsibilities.

Above all, perhaps, there is now the growing realisation among art dealers and auctioneers that there is indeed something specially dubious about illicit antiquities. They are not at all the same as Old Masters or Impressionist Paintings, and they always bring with them special problems. Inevitably the trade in illicit antiquities is sleazy. And it has been giving a bad name to the entire commercial art world in London, New York and Switzerland. One former British government minister remarked privately to me that the London antiquities dealing scene had become a 'thieves' kitchen'. It was for that reason perhaps that Sotheby's in 1997 decided to set up a inquiry into its London antiquities sales operation and subsequently opted to cease dealing altogether in London in the field of antiquities. The awareness is developing that there is something inherently unsavoury about dealing in unprovenanced antiquities, and at last, perhaps, that there is even something morally dubious about collecting such antiquities.

6

Antiquities in Britain: the local view

Just about every country in the world now suffers from the problem of the illicit excavation and the illegal export of antiquities. Surprisingly, perhaps, Britain and the United States, two of the worst offenders in the open sale of antiquities which have been looted overseas, are not themselves well protected against the commercial exploitation of antiquities uncovered upon their own land. In the United States very few archaeological sites are to be found upon the Register of Historic Sites, most of which date from the colonial era or from the past two centuries. This means that only those ancient sites located upon federally owned land are protected. One of the greatest anomalies in the archaeological world is the freedom with which a landowner in the United States may take a bulldozer to an ancient site, for instance in the American Southwest, and destroy it in order to locate ancient pots for sale. One of the most visually striking ceramic styles in the world is seen on Mimbres Ware (LeBlanc 1983). Yet relatively few pieces come from properly documented excavations, and the majority of Mimbres pots in the museums of America have come from unpublished excavations. It would not be correct to call these clandestine, since they have been conducted brazenly without concealment. Nor in a sense is it looting when a landowner leases his own land out to a professional pot hunter and allows an ancient site to be bulldozed for profit. But the effect is the same.

In Britain the legal position is not dissimilar. There is of course a national system of 'scheduling' Ancient Monuments. Once an ancient site is declared by the Secretary of State to be listed in the Schedule of Ancient Monuments (and hence 'scheduled'), it is protected by law. But other, unscheduled, sites are not legally protected, and it would not be illegal for the landowner to destroy them in the same manner as do American pot hunters. Until recently, however, they have been protected by simple market forces, in that British antiquities, other than those of gold and silver, rarely had commercial value. This situation is now beginning to change – neolithic polished stone axes and palaeolithic 'handaxes' are beginning to fetch appreciable sums in the saleroom.

In England and Wales the position was for centuries safeguarded by the law relating to 'Treasure Trove', which provided that buried treasure of gold and silver should be surrendered to the Crown, following a coroner's inquest to determine whether or not it had been deliberately buried with the intention of recovery. Gold and silver objects which had simply been lost were regarded as the property of the landowner. The Treasure Trove procedure had for many years been accompanied by the convention that the finder, who was obliged by law to declare the find, would receive a reward equivalent to the market value of the finds if these were indeed declared to be Treasure Trove and if they were pre-empted by the Crown (which often in effect meant that they would go to the British Museum). In 1996 the Treasure Act revised the procedure in England and Wales, scrapping the cumbersome requirement that a verdict be reached as to whether or not the objects of precious metal had been deliberately buried with the intention of recovery. It also extended the definition of 'Treasure' (see Appendix 8) to include hoards of more than ten coins, even if these were of bronze rather than silver or gold. This system, which came into effect in England, Wales and Northern Ireland in 1997, works ex-

82

tremely well for gold and silver precisely because the reward system itself operates well, and the finder really is awarded the market value of the finds (see DCMS 2000a). There is thus no incentive to hide them. Indeed to do so denies the finder any entitlement to a reward. But it falls far short of a national antiquities legislation, since it currently applies only to finds of gold and silver (and groups of bronze coins of ten or more). Scotland has its own, more comprehensive legislation which applies to any antiquities found in the land if they are not otherwise owned (Saville 2000).

The rise of the metal detectorist in
England and Wales

For many years the Treasure Trove legislation worked very well in England (despite the anomaly about whether or not the finds had been deliberately buried). The situation was satisfactory precisely because the Treasure Trove law operated in much the same way as the more enlightened antiquities legislation of other countries. The situation has changed over the past thirty years, however, for two reasons. The first is that other categories of local antiquity as now becoming valuable – flint 'hand-axes' from the Old Stone Age, neolithic polished axes, bronze figurines and other objects from the Iron Age, Anglo-Saxon brooches and glass vessels from the early years of the Christian era. All these have now attained a significant market value, and are consequently seen as worth owning and selling.

The second reason is the rise of the metal detectorists. The technology for detecting underground metal objects was a spin-off from methods developed during the Second World War to detect buried landmines. In the 1960s and 1970s it came to be applied in England to the detection of buried metal objects as a weekend pastime, and very soon became widely popular. Most of the finds were, of course, surface finds, including coins, brooches and ornaments as well as iron nails and very fragmentary artefacts. Archaeologists were perhaps slow to realise the threat to archaeological sites posed by the new technology, and on privately owned land the practice is not illegal (so long as it is conducted with the permission of the landowner). It was clear that very many finds of antiquities were being made, most of them perfectly legally, but that absolutely no record of them was being kept. There was no mechanism for publishing them, and no reason for doing so. It should be stressed that most metal detectorists behave perfectly reputably, obtaining the permission of the landowner before using their detectors, and in recent years reporting their finds under the Recording Scheme mentioned below. But there is a small band of 'nighthawks' (i.e. looters) who operate clandestinely and illegally and, as in the case of the Salisbury Hoard (see below), do a great deal of damage.

In 1997 a new Portable Antiquities Recording Scheme was initiated, first as a pilot scheme, involving the voluntary reporting by those finding antiquities to local Finds Liaison Officers. Working initially in just a few counties of England, it has grown to cover more than half of England and Wales and may soon extend over the whole area. (Scotland is not covered since, as noted above, the law is different there and in theory all antiquities found belong to the Crown, although it is clear that such a scheme would be beneficial in Scotland also.) More than 13,000 objects were recorded by the Finds Liaison Officers in the first year of the scheme, and a further 20,000 in the second year, out of the many more which were reported to them.

It is clear that this voluntary reporting scheme is working well (DCMS 2000b), and valuable information is flowing in about the antiquities finds currently being made, not all of which come from the activities of the metal detectorists. The UK Government's role in supporting this scheme is a positive one, in marked contrast to its remarkable and reprehensible inaction over the open sale in England of unprovenanced antiquities from overseas, as further noted below.

In theory the export of antiquities from Britain, or at least those originating either in the United Kingdom or in European Community countries (see Appendix 9), is controlled by law through the export licensing system (DNH 1997). In practice, however, this scheme does not work well, even for British antiquities, and it has become clear that vast numbers of minor antiquities (and some major ones) are leaving without a licence being sought for them.

This is well illustrated by the case of the Salisbury Hoard, discussed below, and by that of the Icklingham Bronzes. These important bronze sculptures from the Roman period were looted by metal detectorists from the farm of John Browning in Suffolk, England, some time prior to 1989. They were exported illegally (i.e. in contravention of the legislation pertaining to export licences), and turned up in the Ariadne Galleries in New York, who subsequently sold them to the those wealthy and well-known collectors Leon Levy and Shelby White (see above). Mr Browning tried and failed to get them back, and was told by the British Museum 'that my biggest problem in trying to recover the Icklingham Bronzes was the United Kingdom's non-ratification of the seriously needed 1970 UNESCO Convention' (Browning 1995, 146).

The Salisbury Hoard

The nature of the problem presented by the open market in antiquities in Britain is illustrated by the extraordinary story of the Salisbury Hoard, well told in the book of the same name (Stead 1998), which at times reads more like a racy 'whodunnit' than a non-fiction archaeological narrative. Again Britain's failure to ratify the 1970 UNESCO Convention means that there is no procedure by which the items of the hoard which have been sold overseas can be recovered.

The story begins promisingly with the sale to the British Museum from what one might have thought would have been an impeccable source – Lord McAlpine, a peer of the realm, once Treasurer of the Conservative Party – of some rather strange and hitherto unrecorded antiquities, a series of 22 bronze miniature shields from the British Iron Age. They were of such evident rarity that a price of £55,000 was agreed. But it soon became apparent that these curious items were part of a much larger hoard, a spectacular find of prehistoric metalwork, which came to be called the 'Salisbury Hoard'. Ian Stead, who was at that time the principal specialist on the Iron Age at the British Museum, set himself the task of investigating the circumstances of the find and of tracing the remainder of the loot. For loot it was. It soon became clear that the hoard had been discovered by 'nighthawks', members of that clandestine fraternity of illicit metal-detectorists who go secretly and illegally by night onto private land in search of marketable antiquities. These they conceal and sell in secret to dealers who do not enquire too deeply into the source of the by-now unprovenanced antiquities. These dealers in turn sell the antiquities on to dealers of better public repute, but who somehow on occasion likewise avoid asking too many awkward questions about the find circumstances and are content to sell them as 'unprovenanced'.

The story took Ian Stead through three premises of reputable dealers, to secret meetings with 'John of Salisbury' in the Red Lion public house in that city, and to the arrest and trial of the two metal-detectorists and the dealer involved. The detectorists were convicted, but the dealer was acquitted on the grounds that he did not know that the antiquities were stolen (although I find it difficult to understand how he could imagine otherwise). Stead was able to re-locate the original findspot and, with the permission of the landowner, conduct a controlled excavation which documented the circumstances of the find. It turned out that this was no ordinary hoard. For as Stead was able to document, the Iron Age shields were part of a very much larger deposit of more than 500 artefacts, which included a series of bronze objects of much earlier date, some of them made more than two thousand years earlier than the latest objects in the find. This must have been a very special deposit, perhaps originally from a shrine or sanctuary (plate 10). The exciting thing is that we do not otherwise *know* of such sanctuaries in Britain, where objects already two thousand years old would be kept and respected, and ultimately buried with more recent offerings. The find has important implications for our understanding how the Iron Age population of Britain themselves conceived of the notion of time and of the idea of antiquity.

In this respect the story had a happy ending. Ian Stead was able to re-establish the *context* of discovery and document securely which objects were found together. As a result the find has important implications for British prehistory. Sold individually these would have been just a few rather interesting objects. But in retrospect was the British Museum right to purchase the bronze shields, which were of course unprovenanced antiquities, in the first place? And it certainly lost out financially as a result. For when it emerged that the original owner of the land where the finds were made (and hence their rightful owner) had been deprived of her property, the British Museum felt obliged to hand them back to her without waiting for any formal legal claims. But when it turned to Lord McAlpine to ask for its money back, no encouraging reply was received and certainly no money. The finds are however of such importance that the British Museum subsequently encouraged the owner herself to sell them (or, as it turned out, to make them available in lieu of Inheritance Tax) which means that the British Museum has had in effect to buy them twice over: once

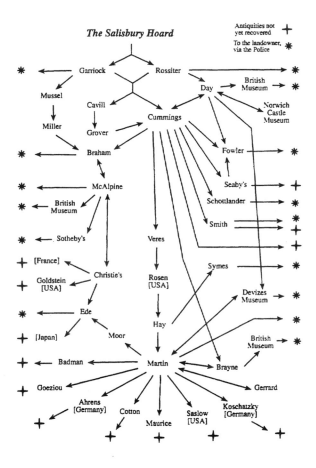

Fig. 2. Chart illustrating the distribution routes of some of the artifacts from the Salisbury Hoard. The initial looters were Garriock and Rossiter, and they sold much of the material to the dealer Cummings. Despite the obviously unprovenanced nature of the material, some of it passed through the hands of well-known dealers (Seaby's, McAlpine, Ede, Symes) and auction houses (Sotheby's, Christie's). (From Stead 1998, 74, fig. 6.)

from Lord McAlpine and then once again from the rightful original owner, i.e. the landowner, after first handing them back to her.

As a spin-off from his investigation, Ian Stead was able to study how the various finds from the hoard had passed through the British antiquities trade following their original discovery by the 'nighthawks' Garriock and Rossiter and their dispersal by the first dealer in the chain (Cummings), subsequently acquitted by the trial judge of wrongdoing (Fig. 2).

This diagram gives a valuable insight into the way unprovenanced antiquities are handled by the antiquities trade in England. Many of the names on the list are well-known dealers (Seaby's, Symes, Ede, McAlpine) and auction houses (Sotheby's, Christie's). It should be stressed that when it became clear that the antiquities had been stolen and were the subject of a police inquiry, all of these cooperated in a perfectly proper way. But each must clearly have understood earlier that they were dealing in unprovenanced antiquities (which is not, of course, currently illegal under British law). Most of them claim to follow 'Codes of Practice' which would prohibit them from knowingly dealing in stolen or looted antiquities. Yet, unknowingly no doubt, that is precisely what they were in reality doing. Moreover many of the finds ended up overseas, and it is to be doubted whether many of them had export licences. That is however difficult to investigate since the Export Licensing Unit of the Department of Culture, Media and Sport makes a practice of declining to answer questions about specific cases – yet another example of the conventions of secrecy which seem everywhere to envelop the antiquities trade (see Brodie, Doole and Watson 2000).

7

Envoi: the past has an uncertain future

In this book I have done something which is scarcely acceptable in polite society: I have adopted a moral tone. For this I hope I may be forgiven. But I have done so because I believe that you as readers yourselves have a role to play, a role which cannot be accomplished by professional archaeologists alone. It is to expose the hypocrisy of institutions which legitimise and abet the looting process by the willing display of recently acquired unprovenanced antiquities. I believe that only by a significant change in public opinion can we hope that there will still, in the future, be the opportunity of learning more about our shared human past from that heritage of material culture which remains.

The first objective must be to persuade private collectors that, if they really respect and value the past, they should in no case purchase unprovenanced antiquities, and certainly not on the pretext that they are 'giving them a good home'. The most simple principle is to treat unprovenanced antiquities as looted antiquities. Only in a few limited cases will this prove difficult in practice. If private dealers are moved by repentance to dispose of their unprovenanced antiquities they should not do so by sale. Nor will any self-respecting museum outside the country of origin accept them even as a donation, if they are following the Philadelphia Declaration. Instead, if the matter is one for concern, they should return the offending antiquities to

90

a museum in their country of origin, unless the Government of that country agrees to their remaining outside it.

The same principles apply *a fortiori* to museums, nearly all of which are public institutions enjoying tax relief and other benefits, even if they are privately owned. Following the Philadelphia and British Museum examples they should decline not only to buy or receive unprovenanced materials: they should decline even to show them on loan. In similar spirit no government taxation department should offer tax relief on the basis of antiquities given or bequeathed to museums or other charitable institutions. As we saw in the Aidonia case, it is unacceptable that public money should go to reward the looting process. It is a disturbing sign that new institutions are emerging which, like the Miho Museum, show little sign of ethical awareness.

At governmental level, there are strong grounds for legislating against the import of unprovenanced antiquities. There are good grounds also for licensing antiquities dealers. For it is clear that in most cases self-regulation, through nebulous and unenforced Codes of Practice, is simply not effective. And of course every nation should subscribe to the UNESCO and Unidroit Conventions discussed above. Currently 91 national governments have subscribed to the 1970 UNESCO Convention. Unaccountably Britain is not one of them, and thus the unrestricted public sale of looted antiquities continues. Further international action would be desirable, and there are currently moves to set up an International Conference on the Traffic in Illicit Antiquities (see Appendix 10). To that end an international Standing Committee was set upon in 1999 under the Chairmanship of Dr. George Abungu, Director of the National Museums of Kenya, and it is hoped that there will be further progress.

Of course none of these measures could be entirely effective. Probably there will always be a clandestine sale in unprovenanced antiquities, just as there may always be a sale in birds' eggs, even though these are protected by law. That is not, however, an argument for doing nothing.

It is difficult to conclude other than on a note of pessimism. It is true of course that public awareness of these issues is growing. In Britain, as noted above, there are select committees and government committees. But so far they have achieved little. In many countries overseas the plunder and the looting continue apace. It may be that, as at Sipan in Peru, the local population will realise that it is *their* past which is being plundered. They may in some cases see that, if only on commercial grounds, it is preferable that the remains of the past are curated where they are discovered, so that they may interest locals and tourists alike. The growth of tourism in the world means that the sort of antiquities which we have been discussing are often of genuine interest to visitors and can form one of the bases for a tourist industry that will bring work and prosperity to the region.

Ultimately it is a matter of public opinion at a world level. It is you, the reader, and others who likewise value our human cultural heritage, who must help set the standard. It is you who should be protesting to museums and to legislators whenever the looting process is aided and abetted by the public exhibition of unprovenanced antiquities. The professionals – the academics, the museum staff – could and should play their part. But in the last analysis this is a public matter, and the decision is yours.

Appendix 1

The UNESCO Convention

TEXT OF THE 1970 UNESCO CONVENTION ON THE MEANS OF PROHIBITING AND PREVENTING THE ILLICIT IMPORT, EXPORT AND TRANSFER OF OWNERSHIP OF CULTURAL PROPERTY.

The General Conference of the United Nations Educational, Scientific and Cultural Organization, meeting in Paris from 12 October to 14 November 1970, at its sixteenth session,

Recalling the importance of the provisions contained in the Declaration of the Principles of International Cultural Co-operation, adopted by the General Conference at its fourteenth session,

Considering that the interchange of cultural property among nations for scientific, cultural and educational purposes increases the knowledge of the civilization of Man, enriches the cultural life of all peoples and inspires mutual respect and appreciation among nations,

Considering that cultural property constitutes one of the basic elements of civilization and national culture, and that its true value can be appreciated only in relation to the fullest possible information regarding its origin, history and traditional setting,

Considering. that it is incumbent upon every State to protect the cultural property existing within its territory against the dangers of theft, clandestine excavation, and illicit export,

Considering that, to avert these dangers, it is essential for every State to become increasingly alive to the moral obligations to respect its own cultural heritage and that of all nations,

Considering that, as cultural institutions, museums, libraries and archives should ensure that their collections are built up in accordance with universally recognized moral principles,

Appendix 1

Considering that the illicit import, export and transfer of ownership of cultural property is an obstacle to that understanding between nations which it is part of Unesco's mission to promote by recommending to interested States, international conventions to this end,

Considering that the protection of cultural heritage can be effective only if organized both nationally and internationally among States working in close co-operation,

Considering that the Unesco General Conference adopted a Recommendation to this effect in 1964,

Having before it further proposals on the means of prohibiting and preventing the illicit import, export and transfer of ownership of cultural property, a question which is on the agenda for the session as item 19,

Having decided, at its fifteenth session, that this question should be made the subject of an international convention,

Adopts this Convention on the fourteenth day of November 1970.

Article 1
For the purposes of this Convention, the term "cultural property" means property which, on religious or secular grounds, is specifically designated by each State as being of importance for archaeology, prehistory, history, literature, art or science and which belongs to the following categories:

(a) Rare collections and specimens of fauna, flora, minerals and anatomy, and objects of palaeontological interest;
(b) property relating to history, including the history of science and technology and military and social history, to the life of national leaders, thinkers, scientists and artists and to events of national importance;
(c) products of archaeological excavations (including regular and clandestine) or of archaeological discoveries;
(d) elements of artistic or historical monuments or archaeological sites which have been dismembered;
(e) antiquities more than one hundred years old, such as inscriptions, coins and engraved seals;
(f) objects of ethnological interest;
(g) property of artistic interest, such as:

94

(i) pictures, paintings and drawings produced entirely by hand on any support and in any material (excluding industrial designs and manufactured articles decorated by hand);
(ii) original works of statuary art and sculpture in any material;
(iii) original engravings, prints and lithographs;
(iv) original artistic assemblages and montages in any material;

(h) rare manuscripts and incunabula, old books, documents and publications of special interest (historical, artistic, scientific, literary, etc.) singly or in collections;
(i) postage, revenue and similar stamps, singly or in collections;
(j) archives, including sound, photographic and cinematographic archives;
(k) articles of furniture more than one hundred years old and old musical instruments.

Article 2
1. The States Parties to this Convention recognize that the illicit import, export and transfer of ownership of cultural property is one of the main causes of the impoverishment of the cultural heritage of the countries of origin of such property and that international co-operation constitutes one of the most efficient means of protecting each country's cultural property against all the dangers resulting therefrom.

2. To this end, the States Parties undertake to oppose such practices with the means at their disposal, and particularly by removing their causes, putting a stop to current practices, and by helping to make the necessary reparations.

Article 3
The import, export or transfer of ownership of cultural property effected contrary to the provisions adopted under this Convention by the States Parties thereto, shall be illicit.

Article 4
The States Parties to this Convention recognize that for the purpose of the Convention property which belongs to the following categories forms part of the cultural heritage of each State:

(a) Cultural property created by the individual or collective genius of nationals of the State concerned, and cultural property of importance to the State concerned created within the territory of that State by foreign nationals or stateless persons resident within such territory;

95

(b) cultural property found within the national territory;
(c) cultural property acquired by archaeological, ethnological or natural science missions, with the consent of the competent authorities of the country of origin of such property;
(d) cultural property which has been the subject of a freely agreed exchange;
(e) cultural property received as a gift or purchased legally with the consent of the competent authorities of the country of origin of such property.

Article 5

To ensure the protection of their cultural property against illicit import, export and transfer of ownership, the States Parties to this Convention undertake, as appropriate for each country, to set up within their territories one or more national services, where such services do not already exist, for the protection of the cultural heritage, with a qualified staff sufficient in number for the effective carrying out of the following functions:

(a) Contributing to the formation of draft laws and regulations designed to secure the protection of the cultural heritage and particularly prevention of the illicit import, export and transfer of ownership of important cultural property;
(b) establishing and keeping up to date, on the basis of a national inventory of protected property, a list of important public and private cultural property whose export would constitute an appreciable impoverishment of the national cultural heritage;
(c) promoting the development or the establishment of scientific and technical institutions (museums, libraries, archives, laboratories, workshops...) required to ensure the preservation and presentation of cultural property;
(d) organizing the supervision of archaeological excavations, ensuring the preservation "in situ" of certain cultural property, and protecting certain areas reserved for future archaeological research;
(e) establishing, for the benefit of those concerned (curators, collectors, antique dealers, etc.) rules in conformity with the ethical principles set forth in this Convention; and taking steps to ensure the observance of those rules;
(f) taking educational measures to stimulate and develop respect for the cultural heritage of all States, and spreading knowledge of the provisions of this Convention;
(g) seeing that appropriate publicity is given to the disappearance of any items of cultural property.

Article 6
The States Parties to this Convention undertake:

(a) To introduce an appropriate certificate in which the exporting State would specify that the export of the cultural property in question is authorized. The certificate should accompany all items of cultural property exported in accordance with the regulations;
(b) to prohibit the exportation of cultural property from their territory unless accompanied by the above mentioned export certificate
(c) to publicize this prohibition by appropriate means, particularly among persons likely to export or import cultural property.

Article 7
The States Parties to this Convention undertake:

(a) To take the necessary measures, consistent with national legislation, to prevent museums and similar institutions within their territories from acquiring cultural property originating in another State Party which has been illegally exported after entry into force of this Convention, in the States concerned. Whenever possible, to inform a State of origin Party to this Convention of an offer of such cultural property illegally removed from that State after the entry into force of this Convention in both States;
(b) (i) to prohibit the import of cultural property stolen from a museum or a religious or secular public monument or similar institution in another State Party to this Convention after the entry into force of this Convention for the States concerned, provided that such property is documented as appearing in the inventory of that institution;
(ii) at the request of the State Party of origin to take appropriate steps to recover and return any such cultural property imported after the entry into force of this Convention in both States concerned, provided, however, that the requesting State shall pay just compensation to an innocent purchaser or to a person who has valid title to that property. Requests for recovery and return shall be made through diplomatic offices. The requesting Party shall furnish, at its expense, the documentation and other evidence necessary to establish its claim for recovery and return. The Parties shall impose no customs duties or other charges upon cultural property returned pursuant to this Article. All expenses incident to the return and delivery of the cultural property shall be borne by the requesting Party.

Appendix 1

Article 8

The States Parties to this Convention undertake to impose penalties or administrative sanctions on any person responsible for infringing the prohibitions referred to under Articles 6 (b) and 7 (b) above.

Article 9

Any State Party to this Convention whose cultural patrimony is in jeopardy from pillage of archaeological or ethnological materials may call upon other States Parties who are affected. The States Parties to this Convention undertake, in these circumstances. To participate in a concerted international effort to determine and to carry out the necessary concrete measures, including the control of exports and imports and international commerce in the specific materials concerned. Pending agreement each State concerned shall take provisional measures to the extent feasible to prevent irremediable injury to the cultural heritage of the requesting State.

Article 10

The States Parties to this Convention undertake:

(a) To restrict by education, information and vigilance, movement of cultural property illegally removed from any State Party to this Convention and, as appropriate for each country, oblige antique dealers, subject to penal or administrative sanctions, to maintain a register recording the origin of each item of cultural property, names and addresses of the supplier. description and price of each item sold and to inform the purchaser of the cultural property of the export prohibition to which such property may be subject;
(b) to endeavour by educational means to create and develop in the public mind a realization of the value of cultural property and the threat to the cultural heritage created by theft, clandestine excavations and illicit exports.

Article 11

The export and transfer of ownership of cultural property under compulsion arising directly or indirectly from the occupation of a country by a foreign power shall be regarded as illicit.

Article 12

The States Parties to this Convention shall respect the cultural heritage within the territories for the international relations of which they are responsible, and shall take all appropriate measures to prohibit and prevent the illicit import, export and transfer of ownership of cultural property in such territories.

Article 13

The States Parties to this Convention also undertake, consistent with the laws of each State:

(a) To prevent by all appropriate means transfers of ownership of cultural property likely to promote the illicit import or export of such property;

(b) to ensure that their competent services co-operate in facilitating the earliest possible restitution of illicitly exported cultural property to its rightful owner;

(c) to admit actions for recovery of lost or stolen items of cultural property brought by or on behalf of the rightful owners;

(d) to recognize the indefeasible right of each State party to this Convention to classify and declare certain cultural property as inalienable which should therefore ipso facto not be exported, and to facilitate recovery of such property by the State concerned in cases where it has been exported.

Article 14

In order to prevent illicit export and to meet the obligations arising from the implementation of this Convention, each State Party to the Convention should, as far as it is able, provide the national services responsible for the protection of its cultural heritage with an adequate budget and, if necessary, should set up a fund for this purpose.

Article 15

Nothing in this Convention shall prevent State Parties thereto from concluding special agreements among themselves or from continuing to implement agreements already concluded regarding the restitution of cultural property removed, whatever the reason, from its territory of origin, before the entry into force of this Convention for the States concerned.

Article 16

The States Parties to this Convention shall in their periodic reports submitted to the General Conference of the United Nations Educational, Scientific and Cultural Organization on dates and in a manner to be determined by it, give information on the legislative and administrative provisions which they have adopted and other action which they have taken for the application of this Convention, together with details of the experience acquired in this field.

Article 17

1. The States Parties to this Convention may call on the technical

Appendix 1

assistance of the United Nations Educational, Scientific and Cultural Organization, particularly as regards:
(a) information and education;
(b) consultation and expert advice;
(c) co-ordination and good offices.
2. The United Nations Educational, Scientific and Cultural Organization may, on its own initiative conduct research and publish studies on matters relevant to the illicit movement of cultural property.
3. To this end, the United Nations Educational, Scientific and Cultural Organization may also call on the co-operation of any competent non-governmental organization.
4. The United Nations Educational, Scientific and Cultural Organization may, on its own initiative, make proposals to States Parties to this Convention for its implementation.
5. At the request of at least two States Parties to this Convention which are engaged in a dispute over its implementation, Unesco may extend its good offices to reach a settlement between them.

Article 18
This Convention is drawn up in English, French, Russian and Spanish, the four texts being equally authoritative.

Article 19
1. This Convention shall be subject to ratification or acceptance by States members of the United Nations Educational, Scientific and Cultural Organization in accordance with their respective constitutional procedures.
2. The instruments of ratification or acceptance shall be deposited with the Director-General of the United Nations Educational, Scientific and Cultural Organization.

Article 20
1. This Convention shall be open to accession by all States not members of the United Nations Educational. Scientific and Cultural Organization which are invited to accede to it by the Executive Board of the Organization.
2. Accession shall be effected by the deposit of an instrument of accession with the Director-General of the United Nations Educational Scientific and Cultural Organization.

Article 21
This Convention shall enter into force three months after the date of the deposit of the third instrument of ratification, acceptance or

accession, but only with respect to those States which have deposited their respective instruments on or before that date. It shall enter into force with respect to any other State three months after the deposit of its instrument of ratification, acceptance or accession.

Article 22

The States Parties to this Convention recognize that the Convention is applicable not only to their metropolitan territories but also to all territories for the international relations of which they are responsible; they undertake to consult, if necessary, the governments or other competent authorities of these territories on or before ratification. acceptance or accession with a view to securing the application of the Convention to those territories, and to notify the Director-General of the United Nations Educational. Scientific and Cultural Organization of the territories to which it is applied, the notification to take effect three months after the date of its receipt.

Article 23
1. Each State Party to this Convention may denounce the Convention on its own behalf or on behalf of any territory for whose international relations it is responsible.
2. The denunciation shall be notified by an instrument in writing, deposited with the Director-General of the United Nations Educational, Scientific and Cultural Organization.
3. The denunciation shall take effect twelve months after the receipt of the instrument of denunciation.

Article 24

The Director-General of the United Nations Educational, Scientific and Cultural Organization shall inform the States members of the Organization, the States not members of the Organization which are referred to in Article 20, as well as the United Nations, of the deposit of all the instruments of ratification, acceptance and accession provided for in Articles 19 and 20, and of the notifications and denunciations provided for in Articles 22 and 23 respectively.

Article 25
1. This Convention may be revised by the General Conference of the United Nations Educational, Scientific and Cultural Organization. Any such revision shall, however, bind only the States which shall become Parties to the revising convention.
2. If the General Conference should adopt a new convention revising this Convention in whole or in part, then, unless the new convention otherwise provides, this Convention shall cease to be open to

ratification, acceptance or accession, as from the date on which the new revising convention enters into force.

Article 26

In conformity with Article 102 of the Charter of the United Nations, this Convention shall be registered with the Secretariat of the United Nations at the request of the Director-General of the United Nations Educational, Scientific and Cultural Organization.

Done in Paris this seventeenth day of November 1970, in two authentic copies bearing the signature of the President of the sixteenth session of the General Conference and of the Director General of the United Nations Educational, Scientific and Cultural Organization, which shall be deposited in the archives of the United Nations Educational, Scientific and Cultural Organization, and certified true copies of which shall be delivered to all the States referred to in Articles 19 and 20 as well as to the United Nations.

The foregoing is the authentic text of the Convention duly adopted by the General Conference of the United Nations Educational, Scientific and Cultural Organization during its sixteenth session, which was held in Paris and declared closed the fourteenth day of November 1970.

IN FAITH WHEREOF we have appended our signatures this seventeenth day of November 1970.

The President of the General Conference
ATILIO DELL'ORO MAINI

The Director General
RENE MAHEU

Certified copy
Paris,

Director, Office of International
Standards and Legal Affairs,
United Nations Educational
Scientific and Cultural Organisation

Appendix 2

The Unidroit Convention

FINAL ACT OF THE DIPLOMATIC CONFERENCE FOR THE
ADOPTION OF THE DRAFT UNIDROIT CONVENTION ON
THE INTERNATIONAL RETURN OF STOLEN OR
ILLEGALLY EXPORTED CULTURAL OBJECTS

1. The Diplomatic Conference for the adoption of the draft Unidroit Convention on the International Return of Stolen or Illegally Exported Cultural Objects was held in Rome, Italy from 7 to 24 June 1995.
2. Representatives of 70 States participated in the Conference, namely representatives of:

the Republic of Albania; the People's Democratic Republic of Algeria; the Republic of Angola; the Argentine Republic; Australia; the Republic of Austria; the Republic of Belarus; the Kingdom of Belgium; the Republic of Bolivia; the Federative Republic of Brazil; the Republic of Bulgaria; Burkina Faso; the Kingdom of Cambodia; the Republic of Cameroon; Canada; the People's Republic of China; the Republic of Colombia; the Republic of Côte d'Ivoire; the Republic of Croatia; the Republic of Cyprus; the Czech Republic; the Kingdom of Denmark; the Republic of Ecuador; the Arab Republic of Egypt; the Republic of Finland; the French Republic; the Republic of Georgia; the Federal Republic of Germany; the Republic of Guinea; the Hellenic Republic; the Holy See; the Republic of Hungary; the Republic of India; the Islamic Republic of Iran; Ireland; the State of Israel; the Italian Republic; Japan; the State of Kuwait; the Socialist People's Libyan Arab Jamahiriya; the Republic of Lithuania; the Grand Duchy of Luxembourg; the Republic of Malta; the United Mexican States; the Kingdom of Morocco; the Union of Myanmar; the Kingdom of the Netherlands; the Federal Republic of Nigeria; the Kingdom of Norway; the Islamic Republic of Pakistan; the Republic of Paraguay; the Republic of Peru; the Republic of Poland; the Portuguese

Appendix 2

Republic; the Republic of Korea; Romania; the Russian Federation; the Republic of Slovenia; the Republic of South Africa; the Kingdom of Spain; the Kingdom of Sweden; the Swiss Confederation; the Kingdom of Thailand; the Republic of Tunisia; the Republic of Turkey; Ukraine; the United Kingdom of Great Britain and Northern Ireland; the United States of America; the Republic of Yemen; the Republic of Zambia.

3. Eight States sent observers to the Conference, namely:

the Republic of Bosnia/Herzegovina; the Republic of Ghana; the Republic of Guatemala; the Republic of Honduras; the Hashemite Kingdom of Jordan; the Kingdom of Saudi Arabia; the Syrian Arab Republic; the Republic of Venezuela.

4. The following intergovernmental Organisations were represented by observers at the Conference:
the Commission of the European Communities
the Council of Europe
the Council of the European Union
the Hague Conference on Private International Law
the International Centre for the Study of the Preservation and the Restoration of Cultural Property
the International Criminal Police Organization
the United Nations Educational, Scientific and Cultural Organisation.

UNIDROIT CONVENTION ON STOLEN OR
ILLEGALLY EXPORTED CULTURAL OBJECTS

THE STATES PARTIES TO THIS CONVENTION

ASSEMBLED in Rome at the invitation of the Government of the Italian Republic from 7 to 24 June 1995 for a Diplomatic Conference for the adoption of the draft Unidroit Convention on the International Return of Stolen or Illegally exported Cultural Objects,

CONVINCED of the fundamental importance of the protection of cultural heritage and of cultural exchanges for promoting understanding between peoples, and the dissemination of culture for the well-being of humanity and the progress of civilisation,

The Unidroit Convention

DEEPLY CONCERNED by the illicit trade in cultural objects and the irreparable damage frequently caused by it, both to these objects themselves and to the cultural heritage of national, tribal, indigenous or other communities, and also to the heritage of all peoples, and in particular by the pillage of archaeological sites and the resulting loss of irreplaceable archaeological, historical and scientific information,

DETERMINED to contribute effectively to the fight against illicit trade in cultural objects by taking the important step of establishing common, minimal legal rules for the restitution ad return of cultural objects between Contracting States, with the objective of improving the preservation and protection of the cultural heritage in the interest of all,

EMPHASISING that this Convention is intended to facilitate the restitution and return of cultural objects, and that the provision of any remedies, such as compensation, needed to effect restitution and return in some States, does not imply that such remedies should be adopted in other States,

AFFIRMING that the adoption of the provisions of this Convention for the future in no way confers any approval or legitimacy upon illegal transactions of whatever kind which may have taken place before the entry into force of the Convention,

CONSCIOUS that this Convention will not by itself provide a solution to the problems raised by illicit trade, but that it initiates a process that will enhance international cultural co-operation and maintain a proper role for legal trading and inter-State agreements for cultural exchanges,

ACKNOWLEDGING that implementation of this Convention should be accompanied by other effective measures for protecting cultural objects, such as the development and use of registers, the physical protection fo archaeological sites and technical co-operation,

RECOGNISING the work of various bodies to protect cultural property, particularly the 1970 UNESCO Convention on illicit traffic and the development of codes of conduct in the private sector,

HAVE AGREED as follows:

Appendix 2

CHAPTER 1 - SCOPE OF APPLICATION AND DEFINITION

Article 1

This Convention applies to claims of an international character for:

(a) the restitution of stolen cultural objects;

(b) the return of cultural objects removed from the territory of a Contracting State contrary to its law regulating the export of cultural objects for the purpose of protecting its cultural heritage (hereinafter "illegally exported cultural objects").

Article 2

For the purposes of this Convention, cultural objects are those which, on religious or secular grounds, are of importance for archaeology, prehistory, history, literature, art or science and belong to one of the categories listed in the Annex to this Convention.

CHAPTER II - RESTITUTION OF STOLEN
CULTURAL OBJECTS

Article 3

(1) The possessor of a cultural object which has been stolen shall return it.

(2) For the purposes of this Convention, a cultural object which has been unlawfully excavated or lawfully excavated but unlawfully retained shall be considered stolen, when consistent with the law of the State where the excavation took place.

(3) Any claim for restitution shall be brought within a period of three years from the time when the claimant knew the location of the cultural object and the identity of its possessor, and in any case within a period of fifty years from the time of the theft.

(4) However, a claim for restitution of a cultural object forming an integral part of an identified monument or archaeological site, or belonging to a public collection, shall not be subject to time limitations other than a period of three years from the time when the claimant knew the location of the cultural object and the identity of its possessor.

(5) Notwithstanding the provisions of the preceding paragraph, any Contracting State may declare that a claim is subject to a time limitation of 75 years or such longer period as is provided in its law. A claim made in another Contracting State for restitution of a cultural object displaced from a monument, archaeological site or public collection in a Contracting State making such a declaration shall also be subject to that time limitation.

(6) A declaration referred to in the preceding paragraph shall be made at the time of signature, ratification, acceptance, approval or accession.

(7) For the purposes of this Convention, a "public collection" consists of a group of inventoried or otherwise identified cultural objects owned by:

    (a) a Contracting State
    (b) a regional or local authority of a Contracting State;
    (c) a religious institution in a Contracting State; or
    (d) an institution that is established for an essentially cultural, educational or scientific purpose in a Contracting State and is recognised in that State as serving the public interest.

(8) In addition, a claim for restitution of a sacred or communally important cultural object belonging to and used by a tribal or indigenous community in a Contracting State as part of that community's traditional or ritual use, shall be subject to the time limitation applicable to public collections.

Article 4

(1) The possessor of a stolen cultural object required to return it shall be entitled, at the time of its restitution, to payment of fair and reasonable compensation provided that the possessor neither knew nor ought reasonably to have known that the object was stolen and can prove that it exercised due diligence when acquiring the object.

(2) Without prejudice to the right of the possessor to compensation referred to in the preceding paragraph, reasonable efforts shall be made to have the person who transferred the cultural object to the possessor, or any prior transferor, pay the compensation where to do so would be consistent with the law of the State in which the claim is brought.

Appendix 2

(3) Payment of compensation to the possessor by the claimant, when this is required, shall be without prejudice to the right of the claimant to recover it from any other person.

(4) In determining whether the possessor exercised due diligence, regard shall be had to all the circumstances of the acquisition, including the character of the parties, the price paid, whether the possessor consulted any reasonably accessible register of stolen cultural objects, and any other relevant information and documentation which it could reasonably have obtained, and whether the possessor consulted accessible agencies or took any other step that a reasonable person would have taken in the circumstances.

(5) The possessor shall not be in a more favourable position than the person from whom it acquired the cultural object by inheritance or otherwise gratuitously.

CHAPTER III - RETURN OF ILLEGALLY EXPORTED CULTURAL OBJECTS

Article 5

(1) A Contracting State may request the court or other competent authority of another Contracting State to order the return of a cultural object illegally exported from the territory of the requesting State.

(2) A cultural object which has been temporarily exported from the territory of the requesting State, for purposes such as exhibition, research or restoration, under a permit issued according to its law regulating its export for the purpose of protecting its cultural heritage and not returned in accordance with the terms of that permit shall be deemed to have been illegally exported.

(3) The court or other competent authority of the State addressed shall order the return of an illegally exported cultural object if the requesting State establishes that the removal of the object from its territory significantly impairs one or more of the following interests:

  (a) the physical preservation of the object or of its context;
  (b) the integrity of a complex object;
  (c) the preservation of information of, for example, a scientific or historical character;
  (d) the traditional or ritual use of the object by a tribal or indigenous community,

108

or establishes that the object is of significant cultural importance for the requesting State.

(4) Any request made under paragraph I of this article shall contain or be accompanied by such information of a factual or legal nature as may assist the court or other competent authority of the State addressed in determining whether the requirements of paragraphs 1 to 3 have been met.

(5) Any request for return shall be brought within a period of three years from the time when the requesting State knew the location of the cultural object and the identity of its possessor, and in any case within a period of fifty years from the date of the export or from the date on which the object should have been returned under a permit referred to in paragraph 2 of this article.

Article 6

(1) The possessor of a cultural object who acquired the object after it was illegally exported shall be entitled, at the time of its return, to payment by the requesting State of fair and reasonable compensation, provided that the possessor neither knew nor ought reasonably to have known at the time of acquisition that the object had been illegally exported.

(2) In determining whether the possessor knew or ought reasonably to have known that the cultural object had been illegally exported, regard shall be had to the circumstances of the acquisition, including the absence of an export certificate required under the law of the requesting State.

(3) Instead of compensation, and in agreement with the requesting State, the possessor required to return the cultural object to that State, may decide:

(a) to retain ownership of the object; or
(b) to transfer ownership against payment or gratuitously to a person of its choice residing in the requesting State who provides the necessary guarantees.

(4) The cost of returning the cultural object in accordance with this article shall be borne by the requesting State, without prejudice to the right of that State to recover costs from any other person.

(5) The possessor shall not be in a more favourable position than the person from whom it acquired the cultural object by inheritance or otherwise gratuitously.

Article 7

(1) The provisions of this Chapter shall not apply where:

    (a) the export of a cultural object is no longer illegal at the time at which the return is requested; or

    (b) the object was exported during the lifetime of the person who created it or within a period of fifty years following the death of that person.

(2) Notwithstanding the provisions of sub-paragraph (b) of the preceding paragraph, the provisions of this Chapter shall apply where a cultural object was made by a member or members of a tribal or indigenous community for traditional or ritual use by that community and the object will be returned to that community.

CHAPTER IV - GENERAL PROVISIONS

Article 8

(1) A claim under Chapter II and a request under Chapter III may be brought before the courts or other competent authorities of the Contracting State where the cultural object is located, in addition to the courts or other competent authorities otherwise having jurisdiction under the rules in force in Contracting States.

(2) The parties may agree to submit the dispute to any court or other competent authority or to arbitration.

(3) Resort may be had to the provisional, including protective, measures available under the law of the Contracting State where the object is located even when the claim for restitution or request for return of the object is brought before the courts or other competent authorities of another Contracting State.

Article 9

(1) Nothing in this Convention shall prevent a Contracting State from applying any rules more favourable to the restitution or the return of

stolen or illegally exported cultural objects than provided for by this Convention.

(2) This article shall not be interpreted as creating an obligation to recognise or enforce a decision of a court or other competent authority of another Contracting State that departs from the provisions of this Convention.

Article 10

(1) The provisions of Chapter II shall apply only in respect of a cultural object that is stolen after this Convention enters into force in respect of the State where the claim is brought, provided that:

(a) the object was stolen from the territory of a Contracting State after the entry into force of this Convention for that State; or
(b) the object is located in a Contracting State after the entry into force of the Convention for that State.

(2) The provisions of Chapter III shall apply only in respect of a cultural object that is illegally exported after this Convention enters into force for the requesting State as well as the State where the request is brought.

(3) This Convention does not in any way legitimise any illegal transaction of whatever nature which has taken place before the entry into force of this Convention or which is excluded under paragraphs (1) or (2) of this article, nor limit any right of a State or other person to make a claim under remedies available outside the framework of this Convention for the restitution or return of a cultural object stolen or illegally exported before the entry into force of this Convention.

CHAPTER V - FINAL PROVISIONS

Article 11

(1) This Convention is open for signature at the concluding meeting of the Diplomatic Conference for the adoption of the draft Unidroit Convention on the International Return of Stolen or Illegally Exported Cultural Objects and will remain open for signature by all States at Rome until 30 June 1996.

111

Appendix 2

(2) This Convention is subject to ratification, acceptance or approval by States which have signed it.

(3) This Convention is open for accession by all States which are not signatory States as from the date it is open for signature.

(4) Ratification, acceptance, approval or accession is subject to the deposit of a formal instrument to that effect with the depositary.

Article 12

(1) This Convention shall enter into force on the first day of the sixth month following the date of deposit of the fifth instrument of ratification, acceptance, approval or accession.

(2) For each State that ratifies, accepts, approves or accedes to this Convention after the deposit of the fifth instrument of ratification, acceptance, approval or accession, this Convention shall enter into force in respect of that State on the first day of the sixth month following the date of deposit of its instrument of ratification, acceptance, approval or accession.

Article 13

(1) This Convention does not affect any international instrument by which any Contracting State is legally bound and which contains provisions on matters governed by this Convention, unless a contrary declaration is made by the States bound by such instrument.

(2) Any Contracting State may enter into agreements with one or more Contracting States, with a view to improving the application of this Convention in their mutual relations. The States which have concluded such an agreement shall transmit a copy to the depository.

(3) In their relations with each other, Contracting States which are Members of organisations of economic integration or regional bodies may declare that they will apply the internal rules of these organisations or bodies and will not therefore apply as between these States the provisions of this Convention the scope of application of which coincides with that of those rules.

Article 14

(1) If a Contracting State has two or more territorial units, whether or

not possessing different Systems of law applicable in relation to the matters dealt with in this Convention, it may, at the time of signature or of the deposit of its instrument of ratification, acceptance, approval or accession, declare that this Convention is to extend to all its territorial units or only to one or more of them, and may substitute for its declaration another declaration at any time.

(2) These declarations are to be notified to the depositary and are to state expressly the territorial units to which the Convention extends.

(3) If; by virtue of a declaration under this article, this Convention extends to one or more but not all of the territorial units of a Contracting State, the reference to:

(a) the territory of a Contracting State in Article 1 shall be construed as referring to the territory of a territorial unit of that State;

(b) a court or other competent authority of the Contracting State or of the State addressed shall be construed as referring to the court or other competent authority of a territorial unit of that State;

(c) the Contracting State where the cultural object is located in Article 8 (1) shall be construed as referring to the territorial unit of that State where the object is located;

(d) the law of the Contracting State where the object is located in Article 8 (3) shall be construed as referring to the law of the territorial unit of that State where the object is located; and

(e) a Contracting State in Article 9 shall be construed as referring to a territorial unit of that State.

(4) If a Contracting State makes no declaration under paragraph I of this article, this Convention is to extend to all territorial units of that State.

Article 15

(1) Declarations made under this Convention at the time of signature are subject to confirmation upon ratification, acceptance or approval.

(2) Declarations and confirmations of declarations are to be in writing and to be formally notified to the depositary.

(3) A declaration shall take effect simultaneously with the entry into force of this Convention in respect of the State concerned. However, a

declaration of which the depositary receives formal notification after such entry into force shall take effect on the first day of the sixth month following the date of its deposit with the depositary.

(4) Any State which makes a declaration under this Convention may withdraw it at any time by a formal notification in writing addressed to the depositary. Such withdrawal shall take effect on the first day of the sixth month following the date of the deposit of the notification.

Article 16

(1) Each Contracting State shall at the time of signature, ratification, acceptance, approval or accession, declare that claims for the restitution, or requests for the return, of cultural objects brought by a State under Article 8 may be submitted to it under one or more of the following procedures:

(a) directly to the courts or other competent authorities of the declaring State;
(b) through an authority or authorities designated by that State to receive such claims or requests and to forward them to the courts or other competent authorities of that State;
(c) through diplomatic or consular channels.

(2) Each Contracting State may also designate the courts or other authorities competent to order the restitution or return of cultural objects under the provisions of Chapters II and III.

(3) Declarations made under paragraphs 1 and 2 of this article may be modified at any time by a new declaration.

(4) The provisions of paragraphs 1 to 3 of this article do not affect bilateral or multilateral agreements on judicial assistance in respect of civil and commercial matters that may exist between Contracting States.

Article 17

Each Contracting State shall, no later than six months following the date of deposit of its instrument of ratification, acceptance, approval or accession, provide the depositary with written information in one of the official languages of the Convention concerning the legislation regulating the export of its cultural objects. This information shall be updated from time to time as appropriate.

Article 18

No reservations are permitted except those expressly authorised in this Convention.

Article 19

(1) This Convention may be denounced by any State Party, at any time after the date on which it enters into force for that State, by the deposit of an instrument to that effect with the depositary.

(2) A denunciation shall take effect on the first day of the sixth month following the deposit of the instrument of denunciation with the depositary. Where a longer period for the denunciation to take effect is specified in the instrument of denunciation it shall take effect upon the expiration of such longer period after its deposit with the depositary.

(3) Notwithstanding such a denunciation, this Convention shall nevertheless apply to a claim for restitution or a request for return of a cultural object submitted prior to the date on which the denunciation takes effect.

Article 20

The President of the International Institute for the Unification of Private Law (Unidroit) may at regular intervals, or at any time at the request of five Contracting States, convene a special committee in order to review the practical operation of this Convention.

Article 21

(1) This Convention shall be deposited with the Government of the Italian Republic.

(2) The Government of the Italian Republic shall:

    (a) inform all States which have signed or acceded to this Convention and the President of the International Institute for the Unification of Private Law (Unidroit) of:
        (i) each new signature or deposit of an instrument of ratification, acceptance, approval or accession, together with the date thereof;

115

(ii) each declaration made in accordance with this Convention;

(iii) the withdrawal of any declaration;

(iv) the date of entry into force of this Convention;

(v) the agreements referred to in Article 13;

(vi) the deposit of an instrument of denunciation of this Convention together with the date of its deposit and the date on which it takes effect;

(b) transmit certified true copies of this Convention to all signatory States, to all States acceding to the Convention and to the President of the International Institute for the Unification of Private Law (Unidroit);

(c) perform such other functions customary for depositaries.

IN WITNESS WHEREOF the undersigned plenipotentiaries, being duly authorised, have signed this Convention.

DONE at Rome, this twenty-fourth day of June, one thousand nine hundred and ninety-five, in a single original, in the English and French languages, both texts being equally authentic.

ANNEXE

(a) Rare collections and specimens of fauna, flora, minerals and anatomy, and objects of palaeontological interest;

(b) property relating to history, including the history of science and technology and military and social history, to the life of national leaders, thinkers, scientists and artists and to events of national importance;

(c) products of archaeological excavations (including regular and clandestine) or of archaeological discoveries;

(d) elements of artistic or historical monuments or archaeological sites which have been dismembered;

(e) antiquities more than one hundred years old, such as inscriptions, coins and engraved seals;

(f) objects of ethnological interest;

(g) property of artistic interest, such as:
(i) pictures, paintings and drawings produced entirely by hand

on any support and in any material (excluding industrial designs and manufactured articles decorated by hand);
(ii) original works of statuary art and sculpture in any material;
(iii) original engravings, prints and lithographs;
(iv) original artistic assemblages and montages in any material;

(h) rare manuscripts and incunabula, old books, documents and publications of special interest (historical, artistic, scientific, literary, etc.) singly or in collections;

(i) postage, revenue and similar stamps, singly or in collections;

(j) archives, including sound, photographic and cinematographic archives;

(k) articles of furniture more than one hundred years old and old musical instruments.

Appendix 3

The Philadelphia Declaration

DECISION OF THE CURATORS OF THE UNIVERSITY MUSEUM
OF THE UNIVERSITY OF PENNSYLVANIA, 1st April 1970
(from *Antiquity* 44, 171-2).

The curatorial faculty of The University Museum today reached the unanimous conclusion that they would purchase no more art objects or antiquities for the Museum unless the objects are accompanied by a pedigree – that is, information about the different owners of the objects, place of origin, legality of export, and other data useful in each individual case. The information will be made public. This decision was recommended by the Director of the Museum, Froelich Rainey, and also by the Chairman of the Board of Managers, Howard C. Petersen.

The action of The University Museum staff is the result of an increasing illicit trade in cultural objects, particularly antiquities, which is causing major destruction of archaeological sites in many countries throughout the world. Practically all countries now have strict controls on the export of antiquities but it is clear that such controls do not stop the looting and destruction of archaeological sites, probably because high prices paid for antiquities in the international market make it impossible for the countries of origin to stop the movement across their borders.

The United Nations Organization, through UNESCO, is now discussing an international convention which proposes, among other things, that the major importing countries for these objects, such as the United States, West Germany, France and England, should introduce more rigid import controls in order to restrict the trade and protect the archaeological sites in countries such as Turkey, Iran, and Italy.

It is the considered opinion of The University Museum group of archaeologists and anthropologists who work in many countries throughout the world, that import controls in the importing countries will be no more effective than the export controls in the exporting countries. Probably the only effective way to stop this wholesale destruction of archaeological sites is to regulate the trade in cultural objects within each country just as most countries in the world today regulate domestic trade in foodstuffs, drugs, securities, and other commodities. The looting of sites is naturally done by the nationals of each country and the illicit trade is carried out by them and by the nationals of many countries. Hence the preservation of the cultural heritage for mankind as a whole is, in fact, a domestic problem for all nations.

The staff of The University Museum hopes that their action taken today will encourage other museums not only in the United States but in other nations to follow a similar procedure in the purchase of significant art objects, at least until the United Nations succeeds in establishing an effective convention to control this destructive trade.

Appendix 4

'Acquisitions to Museum Collections'

INTERNATIONAL COUNCIL OF MUSEUMS (ICOM) CODE OF
PROFESSIONAL ETHICS, CHAPTER 3 (1995).

3. *Acquisitions to Museum Collections*
3.1. Collecting Policies

Each museum authority should adopt and publish a written statement
of its collecting policy. This policy should be reviewed from time to
time, and at least once every five years. Objects acquired should be
relevant to the purpose and activities of the museum, and be accompanied by evidence of a valid legal title. Any conditions or limitations
relating to acquisition should be clearly described in an instrument of
conveyance or other written documentation. Museums should not,
except in very exceptional circumstances, acquire material that the
museum is unlikely to be able to catalogue, conserve, store or exhibit,
appropriately, in a proper manner. Acquisitions outside the current
stated policy of the museum should only be made in very exceptional
circumstances, and then only after proper consideration by the governing body of the museum itself, having regard to the interests of the
objects under consideration, the national or other cultural heritage
and the special interests of other museums.

3.2. Acquisition of Illicit Material

The illicit trade in objects destined for public and private collections
encourages destruction of historic sites, local ethnic cultures, theft at
both national and international levels, places at risk endangered
species of flora and fauna, and contravenes the spirit of national and
international patrimony. Museums should recognize the relationship
between the marketplace and the initial and often destructive taking
of an object for the commercial market, and must recognize that it is

highly unethical for a museum to support in any way, whether directly or indirectly, that illicit market.

A museum should not acquire, whether by purchase, gift, bequest or exchange, any object unless the governing body and responsible officer are satisfied that the museum can acquire a valid title to the specimen or object in question and that in particular it has not been acquired in, or exported from, its country of origin and/or any intermediate country in which it may have been legally owned (including the museum's own country), in violation of that country's laws.

So far as biological and geological material is concerned, a museum should not acquire by any direct or indirect means any specimen that has been collected, sold or otherwise transferred in contravention of any national or international wildlife protection or natural history conservation law or treaty of the museum's own country or any other country except with the express consent of an appropriate outside legal or governmental authority.

So far as excavated material is concerned, in addition to the safeguards set out above, the museum should not acquire by purchase objects in any case where the governing body or responsible officer has reasonable cause to believe that their recovery involved the recent unscientific or intentional destruction or damage of ancient monuments or archaeological sites, or involved a failure to disclose the finds to the owner or occupier of the land, or to the proper legal or governmental authorities.

If appropriate and feasible, the same tests as are outlined in the above four paragraphs should be applied in determining whether or not to accept loans for exhibition or other purposes.

3.3. Field Study and Collecting

Museums should assume a position of leadership in the effort to halt the continuing degradation of the world's natural history, archaeological, ethnographic, historic and artistic resources. Each museum should develop policies that allow it to conduct its activities within appropriate national and international laws and treaty obligations, and with a reasonable certainty that its approach is consistent with the spirit and intent of both national and international efforts to protect and enhance the cultural heritage.

Field exploration, collecting and excavation by museum workers present ethical problems that are both complex and critical. All planning for field studies and field collecting must be preceded by investigation, disclosure and consultation with both the proper authorities and any interested museums or academic institutions in the country or area of the proposed study sufficient to ascertain if the proposed activity is both legal and justifiable on academic and scientific grounds. Any field programme must be executed in such a way that all participants act legally and responsibly in acquiring specimens and data, and that they discourage by all practical means unethical, illegal and destructive practices.

3.4. Co-operation between Museums in Collecting Policies

Each museum should recognize the need for co-operation and consultation between all museums with similar or overlapping interests and collecting policies, and should seek to consult with such other institutions both on specific acquisitions where a conflict of interest is thought possible and, more generally, on defining areas of specialization. Museums should respect the boundaries of the recognized collecting areas of other museums and should avoid acquiring material with special local connections or of special local interest from the collecting area of another museum without due notification of intent.

3.5. Conditional Acquisitions and other Special Factors

Gifts, bequests and loans should only be accepted if they conform to the stated collecting and exhibition policies of the museum. Offers that are subject to special conditions may have to be rejected if the conditions proposed are judged to be contrary to the long-term interests of the museum and its public.

3.6. Loans to Museums

Both individual loans of objects and the mounting or borrowing of loan exhibitions can have an important role in enhancing the interest and quality of a museum and its services. However, the ethical principles outlined in paras. 3.1 to 3.5 above must apply to the consideration of proposed loans and loan exhibitions as to the acceptance or rejection of items offered to the permanent collections: loans should not be accepted nor exhibitions mounted if they do not have a valid educational, scientific or academic purpose.

3.7. Conflicts of Interest

The collecting policy or regulations of the museum should include provisions to ensure that no person involved in the policy or management of the museum, such as a trustee or other member of a governing body, or a member of the museum staff, may compete with the museum for objects or may take advantage of privileged information received because of his or her position, and that should a conflict of interest develop between the needs of the individual and the museum, those of the museum will prevail. Special care is also required in considering any offer of an item either for sale or as a tax-benefit gift, from members of governing bodies, members of staff, or the families or close associates of these.

Appendix 5

'Acquisition of Antiquities'

STATEMENT BY THE TRUSTEES OF THE BRITISH MUSEUM ON
THE ACQUISITION OF ANTIQUITIES (1998)

The Museum extends its collections by purchase, gift, fieldwork and excavation

In 1998, the British Museum felt the need to re-examine its policy on the acquisition of antiquities. The *Triennial Report 1993-96* stated that the Trustees' policy was to 'refuse to acquire objects which have been illegally excavated and/or exported from their countries of origin'. It was felt that this statement was unhelpfully brief and that there was a need for a fuller exposition of the Trustees' policy. A sub-committee of curators was subsequently established to look at this issue and the following statement was drawn up and approved by the Board of Trustees, July 1998.

Policy Statement on the Acquisition of Antiquities by the Trustees of the British Museum

1. The looting of antiquities for the market, with the ensuing damage to archaeological sites and loss of cultural context, is a practice the British Museum deplores. Archaeological objects are a finite resource and each loss or destruction of their context irrevocably diminishes the world's archaeological heritage.

2. The policy of the Trustees of the British Museum is to refuse to acquire objects that have been illegally excavated and/or illegally exported from their countries of origin. The Museum will make every reasonable effort to ascertain that any object that it acquires, whether by gift, bequest or purchase, has not been acquired in, or exported from, its country of origin in violation of that country's laws.

'Acquisition of Antiquities'

3.   Wherever possible the Trustees will only acquire those objects that have documentation to show that they were exported from their country of origin before 1970 and this policy will apply to all objects of major importance. The Trustees recognise, however, that in practice many minor antiquities that are legitimately on the market are not accompanied by detailed documentary history or proof of origin and they reserve the right for the Museum's curators to use their best judgement as to whether such antiquities should be recommended for acquisition. In doing so the staff of the British Museum will at all times abide by the spirit of the Codes of Ethics of the International Council of Museums and of the Museums Association.

4.   The Trustees recognise the principle that regional and national museums must sometimes act as repositories of last resort for antiquities originating within their areas of responsibility, and they will on occasion approve the acquisition of antiquities without documented provenance where it can reliably be inferred that they originated within the UK, and where such payment as may be made is not likely to encourage illicit excavation.

5.   The principles stated above also apply to the acceptance on loan of objects for exhibition or for conservation.

6.   The Museum does not give certificates of authenticity or valuations.

Appendix 6

'Illicit Trade in Antiquities'

RESOLUTION ADOPTED BY THE COUNCIL OF THE BRITISH
ACADEMY (1998)

1. It is an established fact that the volume and value of the international trade in antiquities has increased greatly during the last twenty years. In some cases this trade is licit, in others it is not. The British Academy believes that the scholarly importance of archaeological and art historical objects obliges it to formulate a stance on the illicit trade in such items.

2. London is one of the principal international markets through which antiquities, licitly or illicitly obtained, pass. The movement of such items may be illicit in one or all of three senses: they may have been excavated illegally or clandestinely, they may have been stolen from their rightful owners before export, and they may have been exported from their countries of origin in contravention of that country's laws.

3. Laws governing the sale of cultural property vary from country to country, and differ even within the United Kingdom. There are various reasons why English law has made it difficult to stem illicit dealing in antiquities. The British Academy is not able to intervene such matters directly. It can, however, formulate principles for the guidance of members of the scholarly community.

4. The existence of a market for illicitly-obtained antiquities encourages the inexpert, uncontrolled, unrecorded and illegal excavation of archaeological sites, the despoliation of standing monuments, and wholesale looting of museums and other depositories and cultural sites. Regardless of the strict illegality or legality of any transaction, this entails not only physical damage to and loss of artefacts, but also an irreparable loss of scholarly information on

126

the context from which they are wrenched. The Academy wishes therefore to express its unequivocal Opposition to the trade in such illicitly-obtained antiquities.

5.   The British Academy notes that the Government of the United Kingdom was not one of the initial signatories of the Unidroit convention drawn up by the Diplomatic Conference held at Rome from 7 to 24 June 1995. The Academy expresses the urgent wish that Her Majesty's Government should continue to participate in all international moves to curb the illicit antiquities trade, and should wherever possible announce their adherence to the spirit of such conventions, whether or not a signatory to them.

6.   A Code of Professional Ethics was adopted by ICOM (the International Council of Museums) in 1986 and published in 1990. By virtue of the membership of the Museums and Galleries Commission's Museum Registration Scheme almost all museums in the United Kingdom are obliged formally to adopt a strict code of practice in this area. The British Museum has a policy to "refuse to acquire objects which have been illegally excavated and / or exported from their countries of origin." Antiquities dealers, as represented by the International Antiquities Dealers Association, have drawn up a code of ethics which in part covers these issues, and to which members of the Association are committed to adhere.

7.   For its part, the British Academy, as a professional association of academics, hereby affirms its adherence to certain principles:

> a) It is inappropriate for an individual to acquire, whether by purchase, gift, bequest or exchange, any object unless satisfied that it has not since 1970 been acquired in, or exported from, its country of origin and / or any intermediate country in which it may have been legally owned (including the United Kingdom), in violation of that country's laws.

> b) So far as excavated material is concerned, it is not appropriate that objects should be purchased or otherwise acquired by individuals where there is reasonable cause to believe that their recovery included the recent unscientific or intentional destruction or damage of ancient monuments or archaeological sites, or involved a failure to disclose finds to the owner or occupier of the land, or to the proper legal or governmental authorities.

127

c) No scholar should be party to the acquisition by his or her institution of the categories of object mentioned in paragraphs a) and b) above, nor to their public display if on loan (except where a national or regional museum properly acts as the repository for items originating within their geographical region, even when deriving from illicit excavation).

d) Written certificates of authenticity or valuation (appraisals) should not be given for objects of doubtful provenance, and opinions on the monetary value of such objects should only be given on official request from museums or competent legal, governmental, or other responsible public authorities. Where there is reason to believe an object has been stolen the competent authorities should be notified.

e) No scholar should be involved directly or indirectly with excavations in contravention of the laws of the country in question, or act as an advisor to such excavations.

Appendix 7

Writ of Summons in the Sevso Case

1990-C.-No._____

IN THE HIGH COURT OF JUSTICE
QUEEN'S BENCH DIVISION

B E T W E E N:

(1) THE MOST HONOURABLE SPENCER
     DOUGLAS DAVID COMPTON
     MARQUESS OF NORTHAMPTON
(2) XYLANDER LIMITED
                         Plaintiffs

                 and

(1) ALLEN & OVERY (A Firm)
(2) PETER HUGH TREVOR MIMPRISS
                         Defendants

_____

WRIT OF SUMMONS

_____

LANE & PARTNERS
46/47 Bloomsbury Square
London WC1A 2RU

Tel: 071-242 2626
Fax: 071-242 0387
Tlx: 8812495
Ref: LAPdeW/MTP/N709.5

Solicitors for the Plaintiffs

129

Appendix 7

IN THE HIGH COURT OF JUSTICE   1990-C.- No. 2266
QUEEN'S BENCH DIVISION

B E T W E E N:

           (1)   THE MOST HONOURABLE SPENCER
                  DOUGLAS DAVID COMPTON MARQUESS
                  OF NORTHAMPTON
           (2)   XYLANDER LIMITED

                                                  Plaintiffs

                    and

           (1)   ALLEN & OVERY (A Firm)
           (2)   PETER HUGH TREVOR MIMPRISS

                                            Defendants

To the Defendants Allen & Overy (a Firm) and Peter Hugh Trevor
Mimpriss both of 9 Cheapside, London EC2V 6AD

This Writ of Summons has been issued against you by the above-
named Plaintiffs in respect of the claim set out on the back.

Within 14 days after the date of service of the Writ on you,
counting the day of service, you must either satisfy the claim
or return to the Court Office mentioned below the accompanying
Acknowledgment of Service stating therein whether you intend to
contest these proceedings.

If you fail to satisfy the claim or to return the Acknowledgment
within the time stated, or if you return the Acknowledgment
without stating therein an intention to contest the proceedings
the Plaintiffs may proceed with the action and judgment may be
entered against you forthwith without further notice.

Issued from the Central Office of the High Court this 8th day of
March 1991.

_____

NOTE:-   This Writ may not be served later than 4
         calendar months (or, if leave is required
         to effect service out of the jurisdiction,
         6 months) beginning with that date unless
         renewed by order of the Court.

_____

IMPORTANT
Directions for acknowledgment of service
are given with the accompanying form.

130

Writ of Summons in the Sevso Case

The Plaintiffs' claim is for damages for:

1. Fraud

2. Deceit

3. Wrongful interference with business interests

4. Negligence

5. Fraudulent misrepresentation

6. Breach of contract

7. Breach of trust and

8. Breach of fiduciary duties

by the Defendants and each of them acting as solicitors and/or
agents and/or trustees and/or on their own behalf in relation to
the acquisition and potential sale of the Sevso Silver and
matters pertaining thereto between 1981 and September 1990.

This Writ was issued by Lane & Partners of 46/47 Bloomsbury
Square, London WC1A 2RU Solicitors for the said Plaintiffs. The
First Plaintiff resides at Compton Wynyates, Tysoe, Warwick CV35
0UD. The Second Plaintiff is a company incorporated under the
laws of Guernsey and has its registered office at PO Box No 186,
1 Le Marchant Street, St Peter Port, Guernsey, Channel Islands.

Appendix 8

The Treasure Act (1996), for England and Wales

Treasure Act 1996

1996 CHAPTER 24

An Act to abolish treasure trove and to make fresh provision in relation to treasure. [4th July 1996]

BE IT ENACTED by the Queen's most Excellent Majesty, by and with the advice and consent of the Lords Spiritual and Temporal, and Commons, in this present Parliament assembled, and by the authority of the same, as follows:-

Meaning of "treasure"

1. (1) Treasure is-
    (a) any object at least 300 years old when found which-
        (i) is not a coin but has metallic content of which at least 10 per cent by weight is precious metal;
        (ii) when found, is one of at least two coins in the same find which are at least 300 years old at that time and have that percentage of precious metal; or
        (iii) when found, is one of at least ten coins in the same find which are at least 300 years old at that time;
    (b) any object at least 200 years old when found which belongs to a class designated under section 2(1);
    (c) any object which would have been treasure trove if found before the commencement of section 4;
    (d) any object which, when found is part of the same find as-
        (i) an object within paragraph (a), (b) or (c) found at the same time or earlier; or
        (ii) an object found earlier which would be within paragraph (a) or (b) if it had been found at the same time.
    (2) Treasure does not include objects which are-
        (a) unworked natural objects, or
        (b) minerals as extracted from a natural deposit.

Appendix 8

Or which belong to a class designated under section 2(2).

2. (1) The Secretary of State may by order, for the purposes of section 1(1)(b), designate any class of object which he considers to be of outstanding historical, archaeological or cultural importance.

   (2) The Secretary of State may by order, for the purposes of section 1(2), designate any class of object which (apart from the order) would be treasure.

   (3) An order under this section shall be made by statutory instrument.

   (4) No order is made under this section unless a draft of the order has been laid before Parliament and approved by a resolution of each House.

3. (1) This section supplements section 1.

   (2) "Coin" includes any metal token which was, or can reasonably be assumed to have been, used or intended for use as or instead of money.

   (3) "Precious metal" means gold or silver.

   (4) When an object is found, it is part of the same find as another object if-
     (a) they are found together,
     (b) the other object was found earlier in the same place where they had been left together,
     (c) the other object was found earlier in a different place, but they had been left together and had become separated before being found.

   (5) If the circumstances in which objects are found can reasonably be taken to indicate that they were together at some time before being found, the objects are to be presumed to have been left together, unless shown not to have been.

   (6) An object which can reasonably be taken to be at least a particular age is to be presumed to be at least that age, unless shown not to be.

   (7) An object is not treasure if it is wreck within the meaning of Part IX of the Merchant Shipping Act 1995.

Ownership of treasure

4. (1) When treasure is found, it vests, subject to prior interests and rights-
     (a) in the franchisee, if there is one;
     (b) otherwise, in the Crown.

   (2) prior interests and rights are any which, or which derive from any which-

    (a) were held when the treasure was left where it was found, or

    (b) if the treasure had been moved before being found, were held when it was left where it was before being moved.

(3) If the treasure would have been treasure trove if found before the commencement of this section, neither the Crown nor any franchisee has any interest in it or right over it except in accordance with this Act.

(4) This section applies-

    (a) whatever the nature of the place where the treasure was found, and

    (b) whatever the circumstances in which it was left (including being lost or being left with no intention of recovery).

5. (1) The franchisee for any treasure is the person who-

    (a) was, immediately before the commencement of section 4, or

    (b) apart from this Act, as successor in title, would have been, the franchisee of the crown in right of treasure trove for the place where the treasure was found.

  (2) It is as franchisees in right of treasure trove that Her Majesty and the Duke of Cornwall are to be treated as having enjoyed the rights to treasure trove which belonged respectively to the Duchy of Lancaster and the Duchy of Cornwall immediately before the commencement of section 4.

6. (1) Treasure vesting in the Crown under this Act is to be treated as part of the hereditary revenues of the Crown to which section 1 of the Civil List Act 1952 applies (surrender of hereditary revenues to the Exchequer).

  (2) Any such treasure may be transferred, or otherwise disposed of, in accordance with directions given by the Secretary of State.

  (3) The Crown's title to any such treasure may be disclaimed at any time by the Secretary of State.

  (4) If the Crown's title is disclaimed, the treasure-

    (a) is deemed not to have vested in the Crown under this Act, and

    (b) without prejudice to the interests or rights of others, may be delivered to any person in accordance with the code published under section 11.

Appendix 8

Coroners' jurisdiction

7. (1) The jurisdiction of coroners which is referred to in section 30 of the Coroners Act 1988 (treasure) is exercisable in relation to anything which is treasure for the purposes of this Act.
   (2) That jurisdiction is not exercisable for the purposes of the law relating to treasure trove in relation to anything found after the commencement of section 4.
   (3) The Act of 1988 and anything saved by virtue of section 36(5) of that Act (saving for existing law and practice etc.) has effect subject to this section.
   (4) An inquest held by virtue of this section is to be held without a jury, unless the coroner orders otherwise.

8. (1) A person who finds an object which he believes or has reasonable grounds for believing is treasure must notify the coroner for the district in which the object was found before the end of the notice period.
   (2) The notice period is fourteen days beginning with-
       (a) the day after the find; or
       (b) if later, the day on which the finder first believes or has reason to believe the object is treasure.
   (3) Any person who fails to comply with subsection (1) is guilty of an offence and liable on summary conviction to-
       (a) imprisonment for a term not exceeding three months
       (b) a fine of an amount not exceeding level 5 on the standard scale; or
       (c) both.
   (4) In proceedings for an offence under this section, it is a defence for the defendant to show that he had, and has continued to have, a reasonable excuse for failing to notify the coroner.
   (5) If the office of coroner for a district is vacant, the person acting as coroner for that district is the coroner for the purposes of subsection (1).

9. (1) In this section, "inquest" means an inquest held under section 7.
   (2) A coroner proposing to conduct an inquest must notify-
       (a) the British Museum, if his district is in England; or
       (b) the National Museum of Wales, if it is in Wales.
   (3) Before conducting the inquest, the coroner must take reasonable steps to notify-
       (a) any person who it appears to him may have found the treasure; and

136

      (b) any person who, at the time the treasure was found, occupied land which it appears to him may be where it was found.

(4) During the inquest the coroner must take reasonable steps to notify any such person not already notified.

(5) Before or during the inquest, the coroner must take reasonable steps-

      (a) to obtain from any person notified under subsection (3) or (4) the names and addresses of interested persons; and

      (b) to notify any interested person whose name and address she obtains.

(6) The coroner must take reasonable steps to give any interested person notified under subsection (3), (4) or (5) an opportunity to examine witnesses at the inquest.

(7) In subsections (5) and (6), "interested person" means a person who appears to the coroner to be likely to be concerned with the inquest-

      (a) as the finder of the treasure or otherwise involved in the find;

      (b) as the occupier, at the time the treasure was found, of the land where it was found or

      (c) as having had an interest in that land at that time or since.

Rewards, codes of practice and report

10.(1) This section applies if treasure-

      (a) has vested in the Crown under section 4; and

      (b) is to be transferred to a museum.

(2) The Secretary of State must determine whether a reward is to be paid by the museum before the transfer.

(3) If the Secretary of State determines that a reward is to be paid, he must also determine, in whatever way he thinks fit-

      (a) the treasure's market value;

      (b) the amount of the reward;

      (c) to whom the reward is to be payable; and

      (d) if it is to be payable to more than one person, how much each is to receive.

(4) The total reward must not exceed the treasure's market value.

(5) The reward may be payable to-

      (a) the finder or any other person involved in the find;

      (b) the occupier of the land at the time of the find;

      (c) any person who had an interest in the land at that time, or has had such an interest at any time since then.

(6) Payment of the reward is not enforceable against a museum or the Secretary of State.

(7) In a determination under this section, the Secretary of State must take into account anything relevant in the cost of practice issued under section 11.

(8) This section also applies in relation to treasure which has vested in a franchisee under section 4, if the franchisee makes a request to the Secretary of State that it should.

11.(1) The Secretary of State must-
   (a) prepare a code of practice relating to treasure;
   (b) keep the code under review; and
   (c) revise it when appropriate.

(2) the code must, in particular, set out the principles and practice to be followed by the Secretary of State
   (a) when considering to whom treasure should be offered;
   (b) when making a determination under section 10; and
   (c) where the Crown's title to treasure is disclaimed.

(3) The code may include guidance for-
   (a) those who search for or find treasure; and
   (b) museums and others who exercise functions in relation to treasure.

(4) Before preparing the code or revising it, the Secretary of State must consult such persons appearing to him to be interested as he thinks appropriate.

(5) A copy of the code and of any proposed revision of the code shall be laid before Parliament.

(6) Neither the code nor any revision shall come into force until approved by a resolution of each House of Parliament.

(7) The Secretary of State must publish the code in whatever way he considers appropriate for bringing it to the attention of those interested.

(8) If the Secretary of State considers that different provision should be made for-
   (a) England and Wales, and
   (b) Northern Ireland,
   Or that different provision should otherwise be made for treasure found in different areas, he may prepare two or more separate codes.

12. As soon as reasonably practicable after each anniversary of the coming into force of this section, the Secretary of State shall lay before Parliament a report on the operation of this Act in the preceding year.

13. In the application of this Act to Northern Ireland-
    (a) in section 7-
        (i) in subsection (1), for "section 30 of the Coroners Act 1988" substitute "section 33 of the Coroners Act (Northern Ireland) 1959";
        (ii) in subsection (3), for the words from "1988" to "practice etc.)" substitute "1959";
    (b) in section 9(2), for the words from "British Museum" to the end substitute "Department of the Environment for Northern Ireland".

14.(1) In section 33 of the Coroners Act (Northern Ireland) 1959 (inquest on treasure trove), for "treasure trove" substitute "treasure".
   (2) In section 54(3) of the Ancient Monuments and Archaeological Areas Act 1979 (saving for rights in relation to treasure trove) for "in relation to treasure trove" substitute "under the Treasure Act 1996".
   (3) In Article 42 of the Historic Monuments and Archaeological Objects (Northern Ireland) Order 1995 (reporting of archaeological objects)-
        (a) after paragraph (10) insert-
            "(10A) This Article does not apply in relation to an object if the person who found it believes or has reasonable grounds for believing that the object is treasure within the meaning of the Treasure Act 1996.";
        (b) in paragraph (11)(a) for "treasure trove" substitute "any treasure within the meaning of the Treasure Act 1996".
   (4) Subsections (2) and (3)(b) have effective in relation to any treasure found after the commencement of section 4.
   (5) Subsection (3)(a) has effect in relation to any object found after the commencement of section 8.

15.(1) This Act may be cited as the Treasure Act 1996.
   (2) This Act comes into force on such day as the Secretary of State may by order made by statutory instrument appoint; and different days may be appointed for different purposes.
   (3) This Act does not extend to Scotland.

Appendix 9

European Council Regulation (EEC)

NO 3911/92 OF 9 DECEMBER 1992
ON THE EXPORT OF CULTURAL GOODS*

THE COUNCIL OF THE EUROPEAN COMMUNITIES,
Having regard to the Treaty establishing the European
Economic Community, and in particular Article 113 thereof,
Having regard to the proposal from the Commission[1],
Having regard to the opinion of the European Parliament[2],
Having regard to the opinion of the Economic and Social Committee[3],
Whereas, in view of the completion of the internal market, rules on trade with third countries are needed for the protection of cultural goods;
Whereas, in the light of the conclusions of the Council meeting on 19 November 1990, it seems necessary to take measures in particular to ensure that exports of cultural goods are subject to uniform controls at the Community's external borders;
Whereas such a system should require the presentation of a licence issued by the competent Member State prior to the export of cultural goods covered by this Regulation; whereas this necessitates a clear definition of the scope of such measures and the procedures for their implementation; whereas the implementation of the system should be as simple and efficient as possible; whereas a Committee should be set up to assist the Commission in carrying out the responsibilities conferred on it by this Regulation;
Whereas, in view of the considerable experience of the Member States' authorities in the application of Council Regulation (EEC) No 1468/81 of 19 May 1981 on mutual assistance between the administrative authorities of the member States and cooperation between the latter and the Commission to ensure the correct application of the law on customs or agricultural matters[4], the said Regulations should be applied to this matter;

European Council Regulation (EEC)

Whereas the Annex to this Regulation is aimed at making clear the categories of cultural goods which should be given particular protection in trade with third countries, but is not intended to prejudice the definition, by Member States of national treasures within the meaning of Article 36 of the Treaty,
HAS ADOPTED THIS REGULATION:

Article 1

Without prejudice to Member States' powers under Article 36 of the Treaty, the term 'cultural goods' shall refer for the purposes of this Regulation, to the items listed in the Annex.

Article 2

1. The export of cultural goods outside the customs territory of the Community shall be subject to the presentation of an export licence.

2. The export licence shall be issued at the request of the person concerned:
   - by a competent authority of the Member State in whose territory the cultural object in question was lawfully and definitively located on 1 January 1993,
   - or, thereafter, by a competent authority of the Member State in whose territory it is located following either awful and definitive dispatch from another Member State, or importation from a third country, or reimportation from a third country after lawful dispatch from a Member State to that country.

   However, without prejudice to paragraph 4, the Member State which is competent in accordance with the two indents in the first subparagraph may not require export licences for the cultural goods specified in the first and second indents of category A1 of the Annex where they are of limited archaeological or scientific interest, and provided that they are not the direct product of excavations, finds and archaeological sites within a member State, and that their presence on the market is lawful.
   The export licence may be refused, for the purposes of this Regulation, where the cultural goods in question are covered by legislation protecting national treasures of artistic, historical or archaeological value in the Member State concened.
   Where necessary, the authority referred to in the second indent of the first subparagraph shall enter into contact with the competent

141

authorities of the member State from which the cultural object in question came, and in particular the competent authorities within the meaning of Council Directive 93/[7]/EEC of [15 March 1993] on the return of cultural objects unlawfully removed from the territory of a Member State[5].

3. The export licence shall be valid throughout the Community.

4. Without prejudice to the provisions of this Article, direct export from the customs territory of the Community of national treasures having artistic, historic or archaeological value which are not cultural goods within the meaning of this Regulation is subject to the national law of the Member State of export.

Article 3

1. Member States shall furnish the Commission with a list of the authorities empowered to issue export licences for cultural goods.

2. The Commission shall publish a list of these authorities and any amendment to that list in the 'C' series of the *Official Journal of the European Communities*[5a].

Article 4

The export licence shall be presented, in support of the export declaration, when the customs export formalities are carried out, at the customs office which is competent to accept that declaration.

Article 5

1. Member States may restrict the number of customs offices empowered to handle formalities for the export of cultural goods.

2. Member States availing themselves of the option afforded by paragraph 1 shall inform the Commission of the customs offices duly empowered.

The Commission shall publish this information in the 'C' series of the *Official Journal of the European Communities*[5b].

TITLE 2
Administrative cooperation

Article 6

For the purposes of implementing this Regulation, the provisions of

142

European Council Regulation (EEC)

Regulation (EEC) No 1468/81, and in particular the provisions on the confidentiality of information, shall apply *mutatis mutandis*.

In addition to the cooperation provided for under the first subparagraph, Member States shall take all necessary steps to establish, in the context of their mutual relations, cooperation between the customs authorities and the competent authorities referred to in Article 4 of Directive 93/[7]/EEC[6].

TITLE 3
General and final provisions

Article 7

The provisions necessary for the implementation of this Regulation, in particular those concerning the form to be used (for example, the model and technical properties) shall be adopted in accordance with the procedure laid down in Article 8(2).

Article 8

1. The Commission shall be assisted by a committee composed of the representatives of the Member States and chaired by the representative of the Commission.

    The Committee shall examine any matter concerning the implementation of this Regulation raised by its chairman either on his own initiative or at the request of a representative of a Member State.

2. The representative of the Commission shall submit to the committee a draft of the measures to be taken. The committee shall deliver its opinion on the draft within a time limit which the chairman may lay down according to the urgency of the matter, if necessary by taking a vote.

    The opinion shall be recorded in the minutes; in addition, each Member State shall have the right to ask to have its position recorded in the minutes.

    The Commission shall take the utmost account of the opinion delivered by the committee. It shall inform the committee of the manner in which its opinion has been taken into account.

143

Appendix 9

Article 9

Each Member State shall determine the penalties to be applied for infringement of the provisions of this Regulation. The penalties shall be sufficient to promote compliance with those provisions.

Article 10

Each Member State shall inform the Commission of the measures taken pursuant to this Regulation.

The Commission shall pass on this information to the Member States.

Every three years the Commission shall present a report to the European Parliament, the Council and the Economic and Social Committee on the implementation of this Regulation.

The Council shall review the effectiveness of the Regulation after a period of application of three years and acting on a proposal from the Commission, make any necessary adaptations.

In any event, the Council, acting on a proposal from the Commission, shall examine every three years and, where appropriate, update the amounts indicated in the Annex on the basis of economic and monetary indicators in the Community.

Article 11

This Regulation shall enter into force on the third day following that of publication in the *Official Journal of the European Communities* of Directive 93/[7]/EEC[7].

This Regulation shall be binding in its entirety and directly applicable in all Member States.

Done at Brussels, 9 December 1992.

For the Council
The President
W. WALDEGRAVE

ANNEX
**Categories of Cultural Objects
Covered by Article 1**[1]

A. 1. Archaeological objects more than 100 years old
Which are the products of:
– excavations and finds on and or under water
– archaeological sites
– archaeological collections

2. Elements forming an integral part of artistic, historical or religious monuments which have been dismembered, of an age exceeding 100 years.

3. Pictures and paintings, other than those included in category 3A or 4, executed entirely by hand in any medium and on any material*

3A Water-colours, gouaches and pastels executed entirely by hand on any material*

4. Mosaics in any material executed entirely by hand, other than those falling in categories 1 or 2, and drawings in any medium executed entirely by hand on any material*

5. Original engravings, prints, serigraphs and lithographs with their respective plates and original posters*

6. Original sculptures or statuary and copies produced by the same process as the original,* other than those in category 1.

7. Photographs, films and negatives thereof*

8. Incunabula and manuscripts, including maps and musical scores singly or in collections *

9. Books more than 100 years old, singly or in collections

10. Printed maps more than 200 years old

11. Archives, and any elements thereof, of any kind or any medium which are more than 50 years old

12. (a) Collections** and specimens from zoological, botanical, mineralogical or anatomical collections;
(b) Collections** of historical, palaeontological, ethnographic or numismatic interest

13. Means of transport more than 75 years old

145

Appendix 9

14. Any other antique items not included in categories A.1 to A.13
   (a) between 50 and 100 years old:
   - toys, games
   - glassware
   - articles of goldsmiths' or silver-smiths' wares
   - furniture
   - optical, photographic or cinematographic apparatus
   - musical instruments
   - clocks and watches and parts thereof
   - articles of wood
   - pottery
   - tapestries
   - carpets
   - wallpaper
   - arms
   (b) more than 100 years old

The cultural objects in categories A.1 to A.14 are covered by this Regulation only if their value corresponds to, or exceeds, the financial thresholds under B.

[†] As amended by Council Regulation (EC) No 2469/96 of 16 December 1996, OJ No L 335, 24.12.1996, p. 9.
[*] Which are more than 50 years old and do not belong to their originators.
[**] As defined by the Court of Justice in its judgement in Case 252/84, as follows: 'Collectors' pieces within the meaning of heading No 97.05 of the Common Customs Tariff are articles which possess the requisite characteristics for inclusion in a collection, that is to say, articles which are relatively rare, are not normally used for their original purpose, are the subject of special transactions outside the normal trade in similar utility articles and are of high value.'

B. **Financial thresholds applicable to certain categories under A (in ecus)**

Value: 0 (Zero)
- 1   (Archaeological objects)
- 2   (Dismembered monuments)
- 8   (Incunabula and manuscripts)
- 11   (Archives)
15,000
- 4   (Mosaics and drawings)
- 5   (Engravings)

- 7 (Photographs)
- 10 (Printed maps)
30,000
- 3A (Water-colours, gouaches and pastels)
50,000
- 6 (Statuary)
- 9 (Books)
- 12 (Collections)
- 13 (Means of Transport)
- 14 (Any other object)
150,000
- 3 (Pictures)

The assessment of whether or not the conditions relation to financial value are fulfilled must be made when an application for an export licence is submitted. The financial value is that of the cultural object in the Member State referred to in Article 2(2) of the Regulation.

The date for the conversion of values expressed in ecus in the Annex into national currencies shall be 1 January 1993.

Notes

* OJ No L 395, 31.12.1992, p.1, as amended by information of 27 March 1993, OJ No L 74, 27.3.1993, p.80
1. OJ No C 53, 28.2.1992, p.8
2. OJ No C 176, 13.7.1992, p.31
3. OJ No C 223, 31.8.1992, p.10
4. OJ No L 144, 2.6.1981, p.1. Regulations as amended by Regulation (EEC) No 945/87 (OJ No L 90, 2.4.1987, p.3)
5. Not yet adopted at the time of this publication; in accordance with Article 11 below, the present Regulation will enter into force on the third day following that of publication of the Directive in the *Official Journal of the European Communities*. [The Council Directive 93/7/EEC of 15 March 1993 is published in OJ No L 74, 27.3.1993, p.74, and produced *infra* p. 387.]
6. See footnote to Article 2(2).
7. The Directive on the return of cultural objects unlawfully removed from the territory of a member State, already referred to in Articles 2(2) and 6, has not yet been adopted at the time of this publication. [The Directive (*supra* note 5) was published on 27 March 1993. Hence the Regulation (EEC) No 3911/92 entered into force on 30 March 1993.]

Appendix 10

The Cambridge Resolution

'TOWARDS AN INTERNATIONAL STANDING CONFERENCE ON THE TRAFFIC IN ILLICIT ANTIQUITIES', RESOLUTION ADOPTED IN CAMBRIDGE, OCTOBER 1999, BY THE INTERNATIONAL STANDING COMMITTEE ON THE TRAFFIC IN ILLICIT ANTIQUITIES.

We, the participants in the Symposium 'Illicit Antiquities: the Destruction of the World's Archeological Heritage' held at the McDonald Institute, Cambridge from 22 to 25 October 1999, hereby resolve that there be instituted an International Standing Conference on the Traffic in Illicit Antiquities (ISCOTIA), whose members shall be the heritage and antiquities directorates of national governments, national and international governmental and non-governmental organisations concerned with the protection of the world's cultural heritage, universities and research institutes in the field of archaeology and conservation, and national and international learned societies and professional bodies concerned with the protection of the world's cultural heritage. We hereby appoint an interim International Standing Committee on the Traffic in Illicit Antiquities with the objectives of (a) organising the first meeting of the Standing Conference, and (b) promoting the aims of the Standing Conference.

Among the aims and objectives of the International Standing Conference on the Traffic in Illicit Antiquities shall be to:

(i) seek the protection of archaeological and historical sites, monuments and landscapes from destruction or damage through public works, commercial developments or unauthorised excavation by looters and others;

(ii) promote the understanding by local communities of their own cultural heritage through education, the development of local museums and site museums, and the organisation of an effective antiquities service in every nation;

148

(iii) institute effective national legislation for the protection of the cultural heritage and the support of international agreements, including specifically the ratification by every nation of the 1970 UNESCO Convention on the Means of Prohibiting and Preventing the Illicit Import, Export and Transfer of Ownership of Cultural Property and the 1995 UNIDROIT Convention on the International Return of Stolen or Illegally Exported Cultural Objects;

(iv) make widely understood that the principal significance of cultural objects and artefacts resides in the information which they provide about the human past, that this information comes principally from their context of discovery as documented by systematic excavation and careful publication, and that such information is irretrievably lost when objects are separated from their context of discovery without full documentation;

(v) seek agreement among museums and private collectors that the appearance on the market of antiquities without provenance is likely to be the result of looting (i.e. clandestine excavation and illegal export) and that it is consequently inappropriate to purchase antiquities without documented provenance (unless these can incontrovertibly be shown to have been known prior to 1970);

(vi) persuade collectors (and museums) that the ownership (and display) by them of unprovenanced antiquities should be seen as shameful and offensive to those concerned for the world's cultural heritage, and that far from according protection to the heritage by curating such antiquities their cash and encouragement promotes the looting process;

(vii) persuade conservators, scientists and scholars that it is inappropriate to undertake conservation work, authentication or scholarly research in connection with unprovenanced antiquities on the grounds that such work ultimately facilitates the marketing of antiquities and hence contributes to the cycle of looting and destruction;

(viii) persuade the tax regimes of national governments that tax benefits should not be accorded to those collectors who donate or bequeath unprovenanced antiquities to museums and other charitable organisations, and to persuade museums that they should not accept donations or bequests of unprovenanced antiquities.

(ix) encourage national governments to protest formally when unprovenanced antiquities originating within their borders are publicly offered for sale in other countries

149

Appendix 10

(x) engage the media of communication to promote effectively these aim and objectives and to expose the 'prestige culture' still surrounding certain museums and wealthy private individuals who continue conspicuously to collect unprovenanced antiquities.

Agreed unanimously by the Symposium, Jesus College, Cambridge on the 24th October 1999

Bibliography

Alberge D., 1999, Sevso Treasure dispute settled, *The Times*, 8 May 1999.

Alberge D. and McGrory D., 2000, Art mole threatens to turn tables on Yard handlers, *The Times*, 29 January 2000.

Ali I. and Coningham R., 1998, Recording and preserving Gandhara's cultural heritage, *Culture without Context* 3, 10-16.

Alsop J., 1982, *The Rare Art Traditions, the History of Art Collecting and its Linked Phenomena*, London, Thames and Hudson.

Alva W., 1995, *Sipan, Descubrimiento e Investigacion*, Lima, Walter Alva.

Alva W., 1999, Destruction, looting and traffic of Peru's archaeological patrimony, in Brodie, Doole and Renfrew (eds.), 140-4.

Andronikos M., 1984, *Vergina, the Royal Tombs and the Ancient City*, Athens, Ekdotike Athinon.

Askerud P. and Clément E., 1997, *Preventing the Illicit Traffic in Cultural Property*, Paris, UNESCO.

Azoy M.L. (ed.), 1981, *Peruvian Antiquities: a Manual for United States Customs*, Washington D.C., Department of Cultural Affairs of the Organization of American States.

Betts J.H., 1993, *Gold of the Mycenaeans. Important Finger Rings, Sealstones and Ornaments of the 15th Century B.C.*, New York, Michael Ward Gallery.

Brodie N., Doole J. and Renfrew C. (eds.), 1999, *Papers Presented at the Symposium 'Illicit Antiquities: the Destruction of the World's Archaeological Heritage', October 1999*, Cambridge, McDonald Institute (precirculated papers: final publication in preparation).

Brodie N., Doole J. and Watson P., 2000, *Stealing History: the Illicit Trade in Cultural Material: Report for the Museums Association*, Cambridge, McDonald Institute.

Bibliography

Browning J., 1995, A layman's attempt to precipitate change in domestic and international 'heritage' laws, in Tubb K.W. (ed.), *Antiquities Trade or Betrayed, Legal, Ethical and Conservation Issues*, London, Archetype, 145-9.

CMS Committee, 2000, *Report of the Parliamentary Culture, Media and Sport Select Committee on Cultural Property: Return and Illicit Trade*, London, HMSO.

Cocks A.S., 1995, The Getty Museum retreats from the antiquities market, *The Art Newspaper* VI no. 54, December 1995.

Coggins C.C., 1969, Illicit traffic in Pre-Columbian antiquities, *Art Journal* 29 (1), 94-8.

DCMS, 2000a, Department for Culture, Media and Sport, *Treasure, Annual Report 1997-8*, London, DCMS.

DCMS, 2000b, Department for Culture, Media and Sport, *Portable Antiquities, Annual Report 1998-9*, London, DCMS.

Demakopoulou K., 1996, *The Aidonia Treasure: Seals and Jewellery of the Aegean Late Bronze Age*, Athens, Ministry of Culture.

Dennis G., 1848, *Cities and Cemeteries of Etruria*, London.

DNH, 1997, Department of National Heritage, *Export Licensing for Cultural Goods*, London, DCMS.

Dorfman J. and Slayman A.L., 1997, Maverick Mayanist: Ian Graham, *Archaeology* September/October 1997, 50-60.

Eddy P., 1998, Hot metal: how an aristocrat lost a vast fortune on treasure that is now worth next to nothing, *Sunday Times Magazine*, 1 March 1998.

Elia R., 1999, Apulian vases, in Brodie, Doole and Renfrew (eds.), 21-35.

Elia R., 1993, A seductive and troubling work, *Archaeology*, Jan-Feb 1993, 64-9.

Flannery K.V. and Marcus J., 1983, *The Cloud People, Divergent Evolution of the Zapotec and Mixtec Civilisations*, New York, Academic Press.

Gado B., 1999. Niger, in Brodie, Doole and Renfrew (eds.), 51-9.

Gilgan E., 1999, Looting and the market for Maya objects: a Belizean perspective, in Brodie, Doole and Renfrew (eds.), 116-29.

Gill D. and Chippindale C., 1993, Material and intellectual consequences of esteem for Cycladic figures, *American Journal of Archaeology* 97, 601-59.

Greenfield J., 1995, *The Return of Cultural Treasures*, Cambridge, Cambridge University Press, 2nd ed.

Bibliography

Hansen R.D., 1997, Plundering the Petén, *Archaeology*, September/October 1997, 48-9.

Haskell F. and Penny N., 1981, *Taste and the Antique*, New Haven, Yale University Press.

He, Shuzhong, 1999, Destruction of the archaeological heritage: illicit excavations in contemporary China, in Brodie, Doole and Renfrew (eds.), 87-94.

Haskell F. and Penny N., 1991, *Taste and the Antique, the Lure of Classical Sculpture 1500-1900*, New Haven, Yale University Press.

Henley J., 2000, Louvre hit by looted art row, *The Observer*. 23 April 2000, 25.

Hodder I., 1991, *Reading the Past*, Cambridge, Cambridge University Press.

Howland R.H. (ed.), 1997, *Mycenaean Treasures of the Aegean Bronze Age Repatriated. Proceedings from a Seminar Held at the Smithsonian Institution, Washington, January 27, 1996*, Washington D.C., Society for the Preservation of the Greek Heritage.

ICOM, 1995, International Council of Museums, *Illicit Traffic of Cultural Property in Africa*, Paris, ICOM.

ICOM, 1997a, International Council of Museums, *One Hundred Missing Objects: Looting in Africa*, Paris, ICOM.

ICOM, 1997b, International Council of Museums, *One Hundred Missing Objects: Looting in Angkor*, Paris, ICOM.

Inglewood, Lord, 1997, Written Answer: Antiquities, *House of Lords, Official Report* 17 February 1997, col. WA 34.

Kaufman J.E., 1996, Getty decides publishing equals provenance, *The Art Newspaper* VI no. 61, July-August 1996

Kaye and Main C.T., 1995, The saga of the Lydian Hoard: from Ushak to New York and back again, in Tubb K.W. (ed.), *Antiquities Trade or Betrayed, Legal, Ethical and Conservation Issues*, London, Archetype, 150-61.

Kokkou A. (ed.), 1993, *The Getty Kouros Colloquium*, Athens, N.P. Goulandris Foundation and the J. Paul Getty Museum.

Kornblut A.E., 1998, Getting to the bottom of split statue, *Boston Globe*, 27 December 1998, p. A30.

Kouroupas M.P., 1995, United States efforts to protect cultural property: implementation of the 1970 UNESCO Convention, in Tubb K.W. (ed.), *Antiquities Trade or Betrayed*, London, Archetype, 83-93.

LeBlanc S.A., 1983, *The Mimbres People*, London, Thames and Hudson.

153

Bibliography

Lee D., 1999, Getty returns three stolen works: curator voluntarily collaborates with Italy in accordance with museum's policy, *The Art Newspaper* X no. 90, March 1999

Leiden, 1999, Rijksmuseum van Oudheden, Leiden, *Ritueel en schoonheid, Antike meesterwerken uit het MIHO MUSEUM, Japan*, Leiden, Rijksamuseum van Oudheden.

Los Angeles, 1996, Los Angeles County Museum of Art, *Catalogue Supplement for Ritual and Splendour: Ancient Treasures from the Shumei Family Collection*, Los Angeles, County Museum of Art.

Mango M.M. and Bennett A., 1994, *The Sevso Treasure, Part One*, Ann Arbor (*Journal of Roman Archaeology*, Supplementary Series no. 12).

McIntosh S.K., 2000, 'The Good Collector', *Public Archaeology* 1(1), 73-6.

Messenger P.M., 1999, *The Ethics of Collecting Cultural Property*, Albuquerque, University of New Mexico Press (2nd ed.)

Meyer K., 1973, *The Plundered Past: the Traffic in Art Treasures*, London, Hamilton.

Mitsotakis K., 1992, Foreword, in L. Marangou (ed.), *Minoan and Greek Civilization from the Mitsotakis Collection*, Athens, N.P. Goulandris Foundation, 10-11.

Nagin C., 1990, The Peruvian gold rush, *Art and Antiques*, May 1990, 98-104 and 134-45.

Ninou K. (ed.), 1978, *Treasures of Ancient Macedonia*, Thessalonike, Archaeological Museum.

O'Keefe P.J., 1997, *Trade in Antiquities, Reducing Destruction and Theft*, London, UNESCO and Archetype.

Ortiz G., 1994, *In Pursuit of the Absolute, Art of the Ancient World from the George Ortiz Collection*, London, Royal Academy of Arts.

Özgen I. and Öztürk J., 1996, *Heritage Recovered: the Lydian Treasure*, Istanbul, Ministry of Culture.

Özsunay E., 1997, Protection of cultural heritage in Turkish private law, *International Journal of Cultural Property* 6, 278-90.

Pal P., 1997, *A Collecting Odyssey: Indian, Himalayan and Southeast Asian Art from the James and Marilynn Alsdorf Collection*, Chicago, Art Institute of Chicago.

Palmer, N. (ed.), 1998, *The Recovery of Stolen Art*, London, Institute of Art and Law and Kluwer Law International.

Pérez de Cuéllar J., 1995, *Our Creative Diversity, Report of the World Commission on Culture and Development*, Paris, UNESCO.

154

Bibliography

Phillips T. (ed.), 1996, *Africa: the Art of a Continent*, London, Royal Academy of Arts.

Politis K.D., 1994, Biblical Zoar, the looting of an ancient site, *Minerva* 5 (6), 12-15.

Prott L.V., 1997, *Comment on the UNIDROIT Convention*, London, Institute of Art and Law.

Renfrew C., 1985, *The Archaeology of Cult, the Sanctuary at Phyla-kopi*, London, Thames and Hudson.

Renfrew C., 1991, *The Cycladic Spirit*, New York, Abrams.

Renfrew C., 1999, *Loot, Legitimacy and Ownership: the Ethical Crisis in Archaeology* (The 21st Kroon Lecture), Amsterdam, Stichting Nederlands Museum voor Anthropologie en Praehistorie.

Renfrew C., 2000, The fallacy of the 'Good Collector' of looted antiquities, *Public Archaeology* 1(1), 76-8.

Renfrew C. and Bahn P., 2000, *Archaeology, Theories, Methods and Practice*, London, Thames and Hudson (3rd. edn.).

Robinson W.V., 1998a, Scholars cite works acquired since 1984, *Boston Globe*, 27 December 1998, p. A01.

Robinson W.V., 1998b, Museum defends artifacts collection; due diligence cited in MFA acquisitions, *Boston Globe*, 29 December 1998, p. B01.

Rose M., 1993, Greece sues for Mycenaean gold, *Archaeology* 46 (5), 26-30.

Rose M. and Acar O., 1995, Turkey's war on the illicit antiquities trade, *Archaeology* 48 (2), 45-56.

Ruiz C., 2000a, Shame on Christie's, *The Art Newspaper* 103 (May 2000), 6.

Ruiz C., 2000b, Bodhisattva in Miho Museum stolen from China, *The Art Newspaper* 103 (May 2000), 6.

Russell J.M., 1997, The modern sack of Nineveh and Nimrud, *Culture Without Context* 1, 8-20.

Russell J.M., 1998, *The Final Sack of Nineveh: the Discovery, Documentation and Destruction of King Sennacherib's Throne Room at Nineveh, Iraq*, New Haven, Yale University Press.

Sanogo K., 1999, The looting of cultural material in Mali, *Culture without Context* 4, 21-5.

Saville A., 2000, Portable antiquities and excavated finds in Scotland, in *The Institute of Field Archaeologists Yearbook and Directory of Members 2000*, 31-2.

Bibliography

Schick J., 1998, *The Gods are Leaving the Country, Art Theft from Nepal*, Bangkok, Orchid Press.

Schmidt P.R. and McIntosh R., 1996, *Plundering Africa's Past*, Bloomington, Indiana University Press.

Schnapp A., 1996, *The Discovery of the Past*, London, British Museum.

Sheets P.D., 1978, The pillage of prehistory, *American Antiquity* 38, 317-20.

Sidibe S., 1995, The fight against the pillage of Mali's cultural heritage, in International Council of Museums, *Illicit Traffic of Cultural Property in Africa*, Paris, ICOM, 109-16.

Sotheby's, 1990, *The Sevso Treasure, a Collection from Late Antiquity*, Zurich, Sotheby's (Auction Catalogue).

Stead I.M., 1998, *The Salisbury Treasure*, Stroud, Tempus.

Thosarat R., 1999, The destruction of the cultural heritage of Thailand and Cambodia, in Brodie, Doole and Renfrew (eds.), 102-12.

True M., 1993, The Getty Kouros, background to the problem, in Kokkou A. (ed.), *The Getty Kouros Colloquium*, Athens, N.P. Goulandris Foundation and J. Paul Getty Museum, 11-15.

True M. and Hamma K., 1994, *A Passion for Antiquities, Ancient Art from the Collection of Barbara and Lawrence Fleischman*, Malibu, J. Paul Getty Museum.

Tubb K.W., 1995, *Antiquities Trade or Betrayed, Legal, Ethical and Conservation Issues*, London, Archetype.

Vitelli K.D. (ed.), 1996, *Archaeological Ethics*, Walnut Creek, Calif., Altamira Press.

Von Bothmer D., 1990, *Glories of the Past, Ancient Art from the Shelby White and Leon Levy Collection*, New York, Metropolitan Museum of Art.

Watson P., 1997, *Sotheby's, the Inside Story*, London, Bloomsbury.

Watson P., 1999, The lessons of Sipán: archaeologists and *haqueros*, *Culture without Context* 4, 15-19.

Yemma J. and Robinson W.V., 1997, Questionable collection, MFA pre-Columbian exhibit faces acquisition queries, *The Boston Globe*, 4 December 1997.

Index

157

Index

Index

Index

Salisbury Hoard, 84-6, 88, **pl. 10**
Schedule of Ancient Monuments (UK), 82
Schick, J., 60
Schliemann, Heinrich, 18
Scotland, 50, 83-4
scholars (*see also* academic community), 10, 30, 42, 46, 75-6
Scotland Yard, 50
Seaby's (dealer), 88, 89
Sevso Treasure, 11, 25, 46, 47, 49-50, 75, 79, 129-31, **pl. 6**
Sheets, P.D., 52
Sidibe, Samuel, 54
Sipan, Peru, 60, 62-4, 92, **pl. 7**
Sloane, Sir Hans, 18
Sotheby's (auction house), 25, 36-8, 46-7, 50-1, 58, 80, 88, 89
St Petersburg, 18
Stead, Ian, 86-7, 89
Stichting Nederlands Museum, 12
Switzerland, 24, 42, 80
Symes, Robin (dealer), 71, 88, 89

Tempelsman, Maurice, 71
Thailand, 58-9, 72
Thosarat, Rachanie, 59-60
Throne Room of King Sennacherib, 56-68
tombaroli (*see also clandestini*), 17
Treasure Act, 82, 132-9
Treasure Trove, 82-3
Troy, 18
True, Marion, 28, 30, 41, 70
Turkey, 25, 32-4, 42, 43, 52, 71, 80, **pl. 3, pl. 4**

UNESCO Convention, 12, 16, 18, 24, 45, 56, 63, 65-8, 78, 85, 91, 118, (*see* Appendix 1, 93-102); United States enactment of, 56; United Kingdom non-ratification of, 85
Unidroit Convention, 19, 66-7, (*see* Appendix 2, 103-17)

United Kingdom, 11, 65, 67, 85
United Kingdom Parliamentary Select Committee, 11, 67
United States, 29, 40, 45-6, 54-7, 61, 63, 65, 71-3, 79-81
University of Pennsylvania Museum, 68, 118-19
unprovenanced antiquities (*see also* illicit antiquities), 9-12, 16, 25, 27-8, 30-1, 34-5, 37-9, 44-5, 49, 53, 68, 70-1, 73-80, 85-7, 89-92; definition of, 9; collection of, 10, 28, 31, 34, 49, 68, 74-5, 78-9; by museums, 9, 16, 35, 44, 71, 73, 79, 92; in catalogues, 10; likely to be looted, 11; purchase of, likely to fund looting, 16
Ur, 21

Venus de Milo, 78
Vergina, 22, 24, 26
Vermeule III, Cornelius C., 33
Vishnu (Hindu deity), **pl. 9**
Vokotopoulou, J., 31
von Bothmer, Dietrich, 22, 25, 29, 33-4, 76

Ward, Michael (dealer), 44-5, 75
Watson, Peter, 15, 38, 51, 58, 89
Weary Herakles (*see also* White-Levy collection), 32-5, 44, **pl. 4**
White-Levy Collection, 29, 32-5, 44, 77
White, Shelby (*see also* White-Levy collection), 28, 30, 32, 34-5, 44, 71, 85
Wilson, Peter, 25, 47, 50
Woolley, Sir Leonard, 21

Xylander Limited, 129-31

Zurich, 9, 24, 48

160